When This You See...

When This You See...
ELAINE REICHEK

With an Essay by David Frankel

George Braziller
NEW YORK

First published in 2000 by George Braziller, Inc.

Works of art by Elaine Reichek are © Elaine Reichek
"…Remember Me" © 2000 by David Frankel
Notes © 2000 by Elaine Reichek

The epigraph is from Marta Morazzoni's *The Invention of Truth*,
trans. M. J. Fitzgerald (Hopewell, N.J.: The Ecco Press, 1995).

For information, please address the publisher:
George Braziller, Inc.
171 Madison Avenue
New York, New York 10016

Library of Congress Cataloging-in-Publication Data:
Reichek, Elaine.
    When this you see— / Elaine Reichek ; with an essay
by David Frankel.—1st ed.
        p.   cm.
    Includes bibliographical references.
    ISBN 0-8075-1460-2
        1. Reichek, Elaine—Catalogs. 2. Embroidery—
United States—History—20th century—Catalogs. I.
Frankel, David, 1954– II. Title.

NK9298.R45 A4 2000
746.44'0433'092—dc21   99-059690

Designed by Rita Lascaro
Printed in Hong Kong

FIRST EDITION

ACKNOWLEDGMENTS

My thanks go to David Frankel, for his beautiful essay and
other contributions, and to David Gray, who has been indis-
pensable to me.

    To George Braziller, who understood that *When This You
See...* could be a book; and Mary Taveras, Rita Lascaro, and
Steven Schoenfelder, who worked to make it one. The Nicole
Klagsbrun Gallery, New York, has generously supported this
project.

    To Beth Handler, who curated the exhibition of *When
This You See...* at The Museum of Modern Art, New York,
and Fereshteh Daftari, Laura Hoptman, Carolyn Lanchner,
Robert Storr, Lilian Tone, and Anne Umland, at the same
institution. For past and future presentations of the exhibi-
tion I am indebted to Lisa Corrin and Julia Peyton-Jones
(The Serpentine Gallery, London) and to Piet Coessens and
Marie-Thérèse Champesme (Palais des Beaux-Arts,
Brussels).

    And finally to my family, friends, and visitors to the stu-
dio: Bill Arning, Elizabeth Baker, Holly Brubach, Melva
Bucksbaum, Leslie Camhi, May Castleberry, Lynne Cooke,
Holland Cotter, Edward J. Davis, Donna De Salvo, James
Engel, Laura Engel, John and Diana Engel, Margery Engel,
Michael Fitzgerald, John Fried, Barry Frier, Kristen Galvin,
Donna Ghelerter, Jo Anna Isaak, Isaac Julien, Norman
Kleeblatt, Anthony Korner, Pat Levenson, Judith Mastai,
Mark Nash, Edith Newhall, Lenore and Melvin Oremland,
Anna O'Sullivan, Jeff Perrone, Barbara Pollack, Nancy
Princenthal, Rena Bransten Gallery, David Rimanelli,
Daniel Rothbart, Ingrid Schaffner, Martha Schwendener,
Shoshana Wayne Gallery, Jeanne Silverthorne, Andrew
Solomon, Marion Boulton Stroud, Elisabeth and Herbert
Sussman, Olga Viso, Simon Watson, and Matthew
Yokobosky.

CONTENTS

Masters of embroidery know that it is not enough to follow faithfully the drawing traced: the expert needlewoman must be in possession of the nature of the drawing, to give to it with each stitch the appearance of life, sometimes life itself. The vibration of a wave lies not only in the perfect placing of the woolen thread, and the passing of the needle in the cloth follows an interior movement that is not exhausted by the mechanical gesture.

—Marta Morazzoni, *The Invention of Truth*

...REMEMBER ME

by David Frankel

Think of a room: it has green walls the color of old libraries, it has moldings, it is carpeted, it is hung with framed embroideries; it is a soft and solemn place.

Yet the room is full of people.

Over there is a visitation from Greek myth: Arachne is consoling Philomela, her partner in the trauma of metamorphosis. Penelope listens in silence, her fingers restlessly unraveling the edge of her wrap, while Hercules, in solidarity, wears a dress. Fable and history confuse: Philomela has a second sympathizer in another woman who, like her, was imprisoned, and tried to escape by embroidering code in cloth—Mary Queen of Scots, the sixteenth-century contender for the English throne. Charles Dickens's Madame Defarge hates the victim role; eyeing the classically reared women with grim impatience, she plots revolt and revenge against tyrants of her own. Off by themselves stand a couple of rough-hewn sailors from Herman Melville's *Pequod*. Apparently a little shy in all this female company, they are holding hands; but Henry James has been attracted to their corner, and is suggesting they leave for a favorite cabaret, the House of Fiction—a place they, too, know well. The architect Adolf Loos frowns disapprovingly, thinking the House should be less ornate; the painter Jasper Johns is counting to ten before saying anything; but Ogden Nash, that witty American poet, seems quite amused. The athlete Rosey Grier, cheerfully indifferent, is doing a parlor trick, balancing a football on a needle. Up near the ceiling is a spiderweb—none of the women seem to mind, but Charles Darwin is taking notes.

And there are more: the Brontë sisters, Charlotte and Emily; Andy Warhol, and the shade of Jackson Pollock; Nathaniel Hawthorne's Hester Prynne—like

Philomela, a woman who made her needle speak of crime; like Mary, a woman disgraced, who made her needle her art.

The room—it is an artwork by Elaine Reichek, *When This You See...*—is buzzing, clearly, with drama and plot. Yet it is library quiet. For even as the words we hear in it murmur and fuse, they spell out silence—the silence of a woman who sits and sews, embroidering the characters of language and image that phrase the characters of fiction and fact. It is through embroidery that Reichek has given her people voice, but embroidery, conventionally, is hushed in the doing, needing unsociable self-contained focus. As work, it is a woman's task of household repair; as pastime, too, it is usually female, excluding the family's men; as art, it is nowhere, really, for we think of art, whether beautiful or ugly, as a philosophical vehicle that will tell us something big, and of embroidery, even when undeniably beautiful, as a decorative entertainment. Yet Reichek knows that embroidery is a language, and that language, even or perhaps particularly when silent, is thought. Or, to quote another voice in her still but articulate archive, the novelist Colette: "I don't much like my daughter sewing....She is silent, and she—why not write down the word that frightens me—she is thinking."

When This You See... contains thirty-one embroideries, most of them based on samplers, the stitchings that, from the seventeenth century into the nineteenth, were common parts of a girl's education. A sampler could be a picture, a pattern, a text, or any combination of these, all drawn in thread. It was a three-in-one tool, teaching a female child, aged as young as six or seven, how to read and count, through the listing of letters and numbers; how to sew, a useful preparation for a life either of leisure (demanding a civilized hobby) or of work (demanding a skill); and, finally, morals, through the spelling out of religious quotations, or of homier sayings and homilies. Grown women sewed samplers, too, making childhood duties a sophisticated practice. But the roots of that practice lie earlier, when embroidery was a pastime for European noblewomen. Mary Queen of Scots, for one, sewed embroideries, and when she was imprisoned by her cousin Elizabeth I, she made her patterns spell hidden messages for her allies to read. (A sampler of Reichek's includes her likeness and initial, the Stuart S, and a motto of hers.) From her time, also, date less finished samplers—rows of disconnected patterns embroidered on one cloth. These samplers in the literal sense were like a dictionary's list of words, collections of syllables stored for future use, to be strung in future sentences, and were passed among women to share what they knew. This usage, too, left its trace on the form.

Many of Reichek's samplers are based on historical examples, which she tailors or copies in most of their details but one: the text, which she replaces with text of her own. Or, rather, with text of her own choice, for she does no writing herself. Reichek's thinking overlaps with that of the Conceptual artists of the late 1960s and the 1970s, particularly in her understanding of art as a linguistic fabric, a grammar. But she is closer to a generation of the later 1970s and the 1980s that, unlike the Conceptualists, wanted pictures—stories, narratives, people. Those artists revived the credit of art as a visual experience, but they hadn't completely lost respect for the older generation, the Conceptual and Pop artists, and they would not (or in some cases tried but could not) resuscitate the 1950s rhetoric of original and originating genius that those artists had rejected. Instead of inventing new images, then, they appropriated preexisting ones, which, however, through recombination and juxtaposition and adjustment, they made give up new meanings. Reichek resembles these artists in that she gives her work the kind of visual richness that in Conceptual art is an optional extra. She also shares the piratical practice of appropriation, for she makes her samplers by sampling—by combining patterns and motifs or lifting whole images from the body of embroidery of all periods that is her legacy, and by searching literature of all kinds for quotations that bear on her subject, which, in *When This You See…*, is the history of sewing, knitting, and weaving, the media of her own art.

Most of the men and women in that still room loaded with speech either sewed, or knitted, or wove, or spoke of these vocations. Among those we have already met, for example, Philomela is the character in Ovid's *Metamorphoses* who is violated by her brother-in-law; although imprisoned and silenced (her tongue torn out), she manages to tell her story by embroidering it in cloth. Penelope, the wife of Ulysses in *The Odyssey*, holds her suitors at bay in his absence by promising a decision once she has finished making a tapestry—which, however, she secretly picks apart at night, while they sleep, undoing what progress she has made. Arachne, too, weaves, but she is rash enough to compete with the goddess Athena, who punishes her impudence (and her skill) by turning her into a spider—the spider, of course, being nature's own weaver, which Darwin studied and James made a metaphor for consciousness. The whalers in Melville's *Moby Dick* weave protective mats for the ship's rigging and masts, and Melville, like James, makes such work an encompassing metaphor. As punishment for adultery, Hester Prynne wears an embroidered scarlet letter, the letter A, which she has sewn herself—although her embroidery, in its beauty, somehow defies the stigma it is meant to announce. Rosey Grier, the foot-

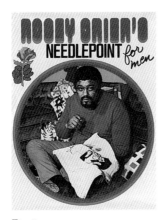

Fig. 1
Cover of *Rosey Grier's Needlepoint for Men* (New York: Walker and Company, 1973)

ball player, wrote a book about needlepoint, his hobby (fig. 1); Ogden Nash, on the other hand, cracked knitting jokes. The Brontës sewed, and needlework recurs in Charlotte's books. Madame Defarge, finally, is the implacable antiheroine of Dickens's *A Tale of Two Cities*, who knits a secret score of the aristocrats named for the hit list during the French Revolution.

Defarge, Mary Stuart, and Philomela seem linked on the same thread in this history, since all of them use their needles to write messages in a struggle with a persecutor. Another of Reichek's subjects, Beatrix Potter, wrote a diary in code, to keep it from her mother, and later devoted one of her children's books, *The Tailor of Gloucester*, to sewing. (Those books, incidentally, pretty though they are, have a Defargean mean streak.) And Reichek copies this code, alongside a letter-perfect embroidery of Potter's mouse, sitting on a spool of silk. The themes of *When This You See...*, then, include secrecy, subjection, and fighting back. Removed from power, and vulnerable to it, women use the arts available to them to stay in the game.

10

Those arts, of course, are not the "high" arts of painting or sculpture, which, traditionally, only men were encouraged to learn; women practiced arts of decoration and utility. But part of the meaning Reichek finds in needlework, and in the stories that gather around it and condition the way we understand it, has to do with what resourceful use women have put it to, and with the range of moods and messages they have asked it to embrace.

Warhol, clearly, had in mind the traditional separation of high art from low in his *Yarn* of 1983, a silkscreen based on a photograph of a textile pattern—but this looping mesh of interlacing line obviously refers to the "drip" paintings of Jackson Pollock. It cost Pollock dearly to invent those images, yet Warhol rhymes them not only with a commercial print but with a domestic accident, a skein of thread a woman might have dropped; he is teasing the Abstract Expressionists, while also probing the nature of abstract art. In an embroidery in *When This You See...*, Reichek returns Warhol's image to its source, by realizing it in cloth. Warhol had translated Pollock's balletic blend of concentration and inspiration into something automatic, quick, mechanical; Reichek reverts to a process of laborious, loving hand labor, but, like Warhol and unlike Pollock, she has no faith in the mystique of spontaneous improvisation, and she works in a medium Pollock would certainly have considered effeminate. Which is surely the point: this, Reichek says, is how women have made art all along. Moreover, the ideas implicit in weaving and embroidery, and the associations attached to them, are culturally pervasive. *Sampler (World Wide Web)* lists everyday words and phrases that depend on these ancient skills, language that extends to the most current technology. Echoes of them also appear in many respected artworks and bodies of art—but, usually, with their female valence hidden or removed. The critical writing on Pollock, for example, often describes his dense beds of line as a "web," and he himself called one of his works *Out of the Web*—and the web, we know, is aligned in our culture with the female, for it is the creation of the weaver Arachne, the girl who turned into a spider.

The links between art thought and needle thought appear in many of Reichek's embroideries. The work on Penelope, for example, *Sampler (Starting Over)*, also quotes the abstract painter Ad Reinhardt:

> Starting over at the beginning, always the same
> Perfection of beginnings, eternal return
> Creation, destruction, creation, eternal repetition
> Made—unmade—remade

Reinhardt is talking about art making, but he could be describing the weaving of Penelope's tapestry. (Her own, less abstract words appear adjoining, telling the story more as—well, a yarn: "I wound my schemes on my distaff / I would weave that mighty web by day / But then by night, by torchlight / I undid what I had done.") The very foundation of weaving and embroidery has a relation not just to art but to contemporary art in particular, in that it is a grid, that crucial idea in modernist painting and architecture. The weaver alloys lengths of thread at right angles to each

Fig. 2
Jasper Johns, *White Numbers*, 1958, encaustic on linen, 28 x 22 in. (71.1 x 55.9 cm). Collection of David Geffen, Los Angeles. © Jasper Johns/Licensed by VAGA, New York, N.Y. Photo credit: Dorothy Zeidman

other, in warp and weft; the embroiderer fits her stitches into the tiny side-by-side rows and columns of square boxes that the weaver has made. And Reinhardt, too, like many other painters from Piet Mondrian to the present, used the rectilinear grid as a structuring principle, in paintings that Reichek reproduces in *Sampler (Starting Over)*. Each of these works is a grid of black squares, the blacks very subtly differentiated—ever so slightly reddish, ever so slightly bluish. Virtuosic as effects of paint, these shifts are also virtuosic as effects of silk and cotton thread.

There are more such correspondences. *Sampler (Jasper Johns)*, for example, is another embroidery based, like *Sampler (Andy Warhol)*, not on a traditional sampler but on a work by a modern artist, in this case Johns's *White Numbers* of 1958—a grid, again, of the numbers from zero through nine, repeating up and down and from side to side, an order self-evident yet absorbing (fig. 2). Reichek pairs it with a girl's traditional number sampler from 1825, a grid of numbers charting the multiplication table. A less obvious Johnsian touch appears in the rulers in *Sampler (The Scarlet Letter)*: Johns has included a ruler in several paintings (*Device*, of 1962, is one example), and Hawthorne tells us exactly the size of Prynne's letter A; Reichek is having fun with a vein of stubborn literalism that is one strain in American art. Similarly, *Sampler (Kruger/Holzer)* places contemporary political and media-related art in a long tradition of American moral voices that found their way into embroidery (fig. 3). All of the samplers in *When This You See...* were conceived to be shown together, as an installation, in the green room with which we began, and that room itself was conceived in dialogue with the modern museum's white walls, the conventional showplaces of contemporary art. And the wonderful bouquets of flowers in *Sampler (The Ultimate)*,

Fig. 3
Barbara Kruger, *Untitled (I shop therefore I am)*, 1987, photographic silk screen/vinyl, 111 x 113 in. (2.82 x 2.87 m). Courtesy of Mary Boone Gallery, New York

Sampler (Ovid's Weavers), and other works are both classic sampler motifs and translations of the floral still life (a staple of painting since ancient Roman times) into another vocabulary, in which the underlying grid of the embroiderer's linen gives a notched angularity to organic forms. We are dealing, we understand, with a sign system, a code for "flower" rather than a naturalistic image—but is there anything natural, really, about painting? And is there any reason why painting, or photography, should condition our expectation of what an image of a flower should be?

Reichek's samplers are images, but they have a special quality. Paint on primed canvas hides the weave of the cloth; in a sampler, the cloth is part of the picture. We see its woven grid. That grid is so tight and small as to be almost subliminal, translating as the grain of the linen, but we are always more or less aware of the tiny scale on which the artist has worked, and of the labor and time at stake in this way of making pictures. Every mark is a stitch, or several, since many embroidery stitches take more than one pass of the needle; every color is a thread, singled or doubled or tripled or paired with a thread of another color to bring it to the right intensity. In that context the chromatic spectrum in Reichek's samplers, the minute detail, the exacting precision of the image, the finely textured surface, all take on a precious weight. And these works are full of carefully figured, often witty touches that may take you a while to notice: the fact that the pattern in *Sampler (Mary Queen of Scots)* includes chains, for example, or that to frame *Sampler (World Wide Web)* Reichek has pictured a word-processing window inside a Macintosh laptop screen.

The overall mood of *When This You See...* is a complex mix. There is humor, with visual jokes like these, or with the revelation of Madame Defarge and the adman Maurice Saatchi as blood kin. There are sad stories and tragic heroines, salted here by a whiff of sea air, there by bracingly cerebral argument. There is a certain sexual undercurrent—we catch glimpses of what happens to masculinity when it bumps up against sewing, and we watch a philosopher flirt. There is the delicacy and elegance of the medium. There are grave presiding presences; one beautiful work is a copy in black and white cotton and silk of a Conté-crayon drawing by Seurat, of his mother, sewing (fig. 4). (The extraordinary thing is how closely Reichek renders the sophistication of Seurat's touch.) And there is another thing: a sense of mortality, of transience, of the passage of life and art into the past, and of their fragile continuity. The title *When This You See...* abbreviates an old sampler saying, a word from the dead to the living: "When this you see, remember me." Reichek quotes a sixteenth-century poet foreseeing his death: "My thread is cut, and yet it is not spun." She sews her name, or her initials, *E.R.*, on some of her samplers, putting herself in the company of the women and girls who have sewn such works over the centuries. Ambitious as Reichek's art is, there is a tempering humility: it knows it is spun out of whole cloth.

Fig. 4
Georges Seurat, *The Artist's Mother (Woman Sewing)*, 1882–83, Conté crayon on paper, 12¼ x 9½ in. (31.1 x 24.1 cm). Collection of The Metropolitan Museum of Art, New York. Purchase, Joseph Pulitzer Bequest, 1955 (55.21.1)

PLATES

with notes by Elaine Reichek

1. *Sampler (Ovid's Weavers)*

ARACHNE WAS A WEAVER WHO CHALLENGED THE GOD-
dess Athena to a contest. The two sat down at their looms.
Athena wove the triumphs and victories of the gods,
Arachne an alternative version: rape, pillage, mayhem.
Enraged by Arachne's tapestry (and also by its quality—it
was as good as her own), Athena picked up a shuttle and
beat the girl nearly to death. But then her heart softened,
and instead of killing Arachne, she turned her into a spider,
weaving for all of time.

Philomela was raped by her brother-in-law, the king
of Thebes, who cut out her tongue and imprisoned her to
keep her from telling. She found a way, though, by weaving her story into a piece of cloth. The king tried to kill her,
but the gods saved her by turning her into a nightingale,
forever singing her sad song.

I used the versions of these tales found in Ovid's
Metamorphoses, that great book of transformation. The mag-
ical process by which something becomes something else is
always the process of art.

Many of the objects in the sampler's lower half meant
something at one time—the acorn, for example, was a sym-
bol of eternity—but most of the meanings have been forgot-
ten. Today they're largely a lost language, but people used
to be able to read a sampler like reading a page of a book.

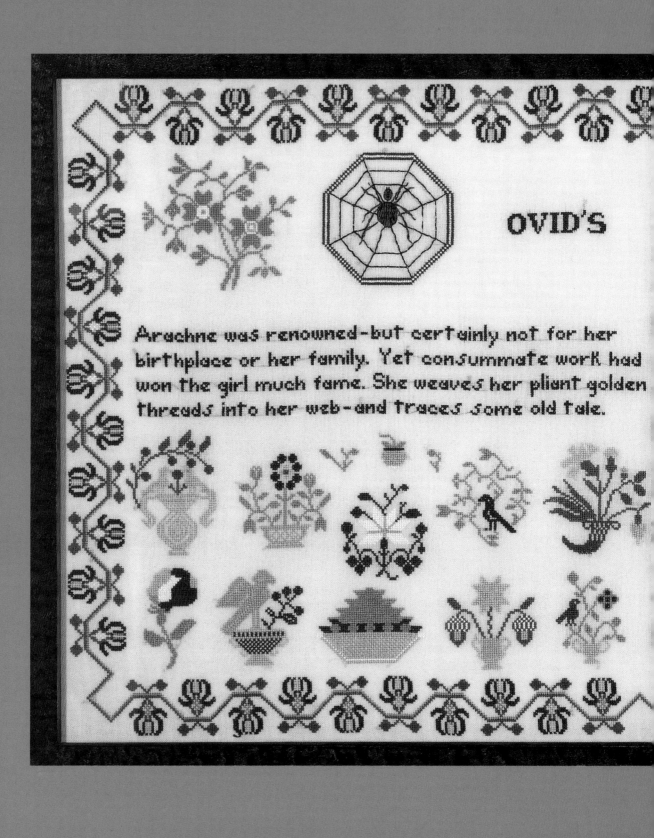

OVID'S

Arachne was renowned—but certainly not for her birthplace or her family. Yet consummate work had won the girl much fame. She weaves her pliant golden threads into her web—and traces some old tale.

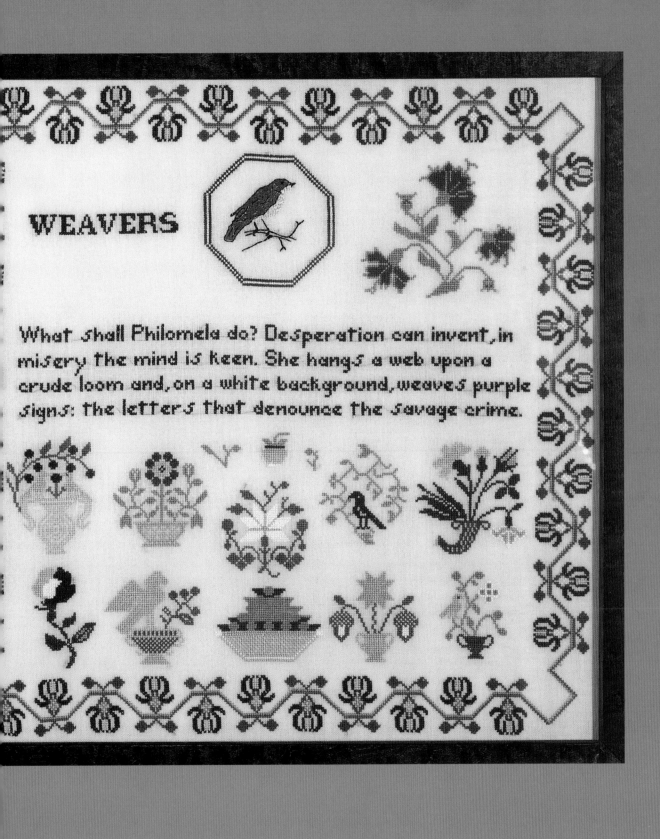

WEAVERS

What shall Philomela do? Desperation can invent, in misery the mind is keen. She hangs a web upon a crude loom and, on a white background, weaves purple signs: the letters that denounce the savage crime.

2. Sampler (The Scarlet Letter)

WHEN I READ NATHANIEL HAWTHORNE'S NOVEL IN HIGH
school, all I really wanted to know, of course, was who had
had the affair with Hester Prynne. Now it seems to me that
Hawthorne is talking about art, and about the artist's place
in society—that in making Hester an embroiderer, he
makes her a skilled and sensitive creator, an artist figure.
He is identifying the artist as a person who in some way
offends the community and stands outside it. The novel
says that Hester is in "a sphere by herself," which I thought
of when I sewed the floral circle.

The Scarlet Letter begins years after Hester's death,
when the narrator discovers in an envelope the letter A that
she had sewn and worn in confession of her adultery. But
the A, I think, symbolizes "author" or "artist" as well as
"adulteress." The narrator goes on to tell Hester's story, and
in the last lines of the book, he looks at her tombstone, a
"simple slab of slate" bearing a device that he describes
with a phrase from heraldry: "On a field, sable, the letter
A, gules." So, for this work, I gave the sampler the vertical
form of a tombstone, and I strengthened that association in
the central box, which, including the rulers at its edges, has
the shape of a cross. I made the letter A red ("gules"), as
Hawthorne did, and the lines in the field around it are
black ("sable"), but they're also a kind of hidden doubling,
because vertical parallel lines are the heraldic code for red.
I wanted to carry that color through, even if in secret.

SHE HATH GOOD SKILL AT HER NEEDLE...

This rag of scarlet cloth assumed the shape of a letter. It was the capital letter A.... Each limb proved to be precisely three inches and a quarter in length.

The SCARLET LETTER, so fantastically embroidered and illuminated upon her bosom, had the effect of a spell, taking her out of the ordinary relations with humanity and enclosing her in a sphere by herself.
— NATHANIEL HAWTHORNE

3. Sampler (Moby Dick)

I ADAPTED THIS DESIGN FROM A MARITIME SAMPLER MADE in New England a little before Herman Melville (1819–1891) was born. I changed the colors, added the rope (it comes from a model-making kit for a whaler), and tied it with a sailor's knot. The original sampler had fanciful dolphins; I replaced them with a sperm whale, which I copied from Barry Moser's 1979 illustrated edition of *Moby Dick*. (Jasper Johns once appropriated a whale from the same book.) I also changed the rigging and shape of the ship, making it a New Bedford whaler of Melville's time. Everything else is close to the original, including the wonderfully out-of-scale flowers. I particularly like the pattern used for the sea—it seems so right that it should be herringbone.

I also love the phrase about "weaving away at the Fates." When Ahab finally harpoons Moby Dick, the harpoon line catches around his ankle, so that when the whale runs, it pulls him overboard and drowns him. This is where the imagery of rope, which is woven throughout the novel, gets tied down. But Melville also relates that imagery to the Fates, ancient mythic goddesses who spin, throw, and cut the thread of a person's life. The idea of weaving, then—"weaving away at the Fates"—is a central metaphor in the book.

MOBY DICK
A Sailor's Yarn

MELVILLE

...God's foot upon the treadle of the loom....

...Thus we were weaving and weaving away...

I kept passing the woof of marline between the long
yarns of the warp, using my own hand for the shuttle
...weaving away at the Fates

4. Sampler (It Was Something)

THE THING I LIKE BEST ABOUT HENRY JAMES IS HIS INTENSE sensitivity to interwoven detail. His prose is intricate, nuanced; his plots hinge on the finest of fine points, and if your attention flags, you'll never make out the pattern. That always reminds me of embroidery—of the countless insignificant stitches that together add up to a whole. In James's short story "The Figure in the Carpet," the narrator examines the weave of a carpet the way an art critic would a painting. He *reads* the carpet.

Sampler (It Was Something) obviously replicates a little Persian carpet. I felt that if I sewed the image in cotton or silk, the usual sampler materials, it would be too regular and wouldn't really look like a carpet; so I used wool. Ordinarily, wool is a bit heavy for fine linen—the thread is too thick for the weave. In this case, though, the way the linen made the wool bunch a little gave me a nice irregular line that I wanted and liked. The line's slight wave makes the carpet look as if it were flying.

Carpets aren't always on the floor—they sometimes hang on the wall, like pictures. But I gave mine a big empty border, so you see it as if there were floor all around it. In art framing, that border would be called a mat, which seemed funny to me in a work about a carpet.

It was something, I guessed, in the primal plan; something like a complex figure in a Persian carpet....to trace the figure in the carpet through every convolution, to reproduce it in every tint...would be the greatest literary portrait ever painted.
    Henry James, The Figure In The Carpet

5. Sampler (The Secret Code)

As a late-nineteenth-century teenager and young woman, the children's-book author and illustrator Beatrix Potter kept a diary in a secret code of her own invention (she didn't want her mother to read it). The diary was translated and published in the 1960s, and on one level it's fascinating—Potter's father was a photographer, and she went around with him a lot, so she talks about going to the art studios and art openings of the nineteenth-century fin de siècle and seeing people like Oscar Wilde. On another level, it's just a daily diary. You have to be a Potter nut to want to read it (though it's fun to read once you start—she was a fascinating woman, and I love her watercolors). On yet another level, this code is so extreme. We think of childhood diary-keeping as benign, but sometimes the writer will fight to keep her secrets.

A lot of children's stories are gentle and sweet, but the best ones, like Potter's, have a degree of the violence that is actually always present in the world. That's why I filled this sampler with sharp things—the scattered pins and needles, the scissors. The mice in the verse are male; Miss Pussy, who offers to cut off the little guys' threads, is obviously female. The triangles in the frame resemble the cut left by pinking shears; they also remind me of teeth.

In illustrating *The Tailor of Gloucester*, which I quote in the sampler, Potter copied the coat that the tailor is making from an eighteenth-century frock coat that can still be seen in London's Victoria & Albert Museum. When she was eight, she knitted a scarf for William Gaskell, the husband of the novelist Elizabeth Cleghorn Gaskell—the biographer of Charlotte Brontë, who is also featured in *When This You See*.... These threads from sampler to sampler are very satisfying to me.

a a L b 2 c O d K e C f
O g 1 h L i L j h k L l
Π m M n C o Δ p Q q W r
Y s 1 t U u V v M w I x
η y 3 z 2 to,too,two 3 the,three
4 for,four 9 and 4 get,2gether

The Secret Code Of Beatrix Potter

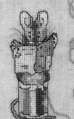

Three little mice sat down to spin,
Pussy passed by and she peeped in.
What are you are at, my fine little men?
Making coats for gentlemen.
Shall I come in and cut off your threads?
Oh, no, Miss Pussy, you'd bite off our heads!

The Tailor Of Gloucester, by Beatrix Potter

6. Sampler (The Little Work-Tables)

JENNY JUNE WAS A CONTRIBUTOR TO THE MAGAZINE *Knitting and Crochet* in the late nineteenth century. I wanted to do something with one of the knitting magazines, because they gave rise to a particular kind of female community. The sewing-circle situation sounds very nice, but today, it's become mostly academic; modern industrial and urban life pretty much erased it. Instead, we got magazines. They were addressed specifically to women and reached a big urban public. Since no man would be caught dead with them, it was as if their readers were an exclusive secret society, a society of lady needleworkers. The Ogden Nash quote recognizes this: just what, you imagine hubby wondering, are these women's fancies? He is outside the circle.

I put in some secrets of my own. The original sampler is homely, even a little ugly, the basic kind of thing you'd find in a knitting or embroidery magazine—a standard pattern. It doesn't include the crossed knitting needles; I added them, as a kind of secret signature. More blatantly, I put the letters of my name in a pink flesh-tone among the letters in the topmost alphabet. I also put in my initials, E.R., at the lower left and gave them a crown. By pleasant chance, I share my initials with the Queen of England, who signs herself Elizabeth Regina. So wherever you see a crown in any of these samplers, it's a kind of ironic surrogate for me.

THE LITTLE WORK-TABLES OF WOMEN'S FINGERS,
ARE THE PLAYGROUND OF WOMEN'S FANCIES, AND
THEIR KNITTING-NEEDLES ARE THE FAIRY-WANDS
BY WHICH THEY TRANSFORM A WHOLE ROOM INTO
A SPIRIT ISLE OF DREAMS.

— JENNY JUNE

Knit 3, Purl 1,
Hubby 0.

—Ogden Nash

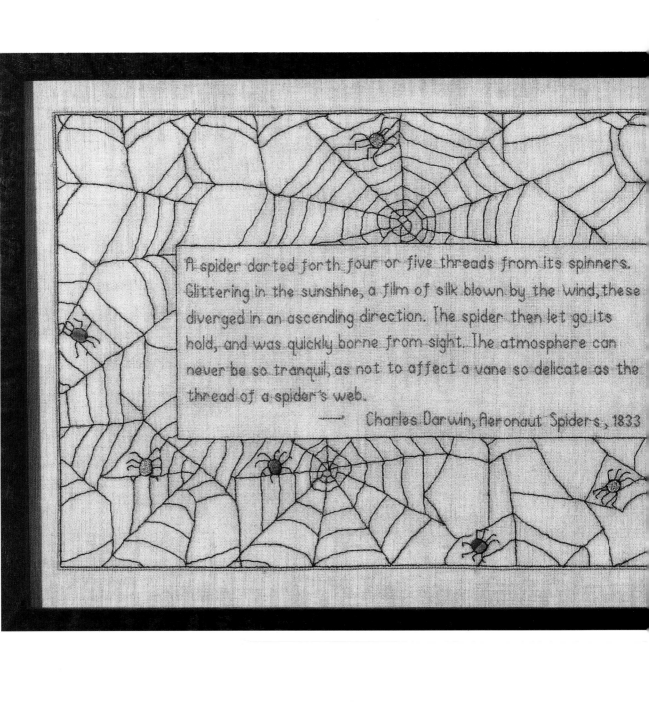

A spider darted forth four or five threads from its spinners.
Glittering in the sunshine, a film of silk blown by the wind, these
diverged in an ascending direction. The spider then let go its
hold, and was quickly borne from sight. The atmosphere can
never be so tranquil, as not to affect a vane so delicate as the
thread of a spider's web.

— Charles Darwin, Aeronaut Spiders, 1833

7. Sampler (A Spider)

I READ CHARLES DARWIN SOME YEARS AGO WHEN I WAS making a group of knitwork and photo pieces about Tierra del Fuego (he landed there during his voyage on the H. M. S. *Beagle*). I thought the writing was incredibly poetic—more so in many ways than the Virginia Woolf quote here, which is quite pragmatic. Darwin is the scientist, but his kind of empirical observation is deeply imaginative; Woolf, on the other hand, is the novelist, but she goes from fiction straight to issues of health, finance, and housing.

The web pattern came from a fabric print, which I redrew and worked into a less obvious repeat. I used metallic thread because spider's silk has a shine to it, and because webs outdoors often have dew on them, which also makes them shine. And I gave the bodies of the spiders body—I made them three-dimensional, building them up with a kind of tufting technique. That was great fun.

I like the way the spiders are dispersed over the web. They seem to be lying in wait, very still, the way spiders do. There's this unsettling mix—the beauty of the pattern versus the menace of ensnarement, the mazelike confusion of the cobweb versus the clarity of the spider's intention.

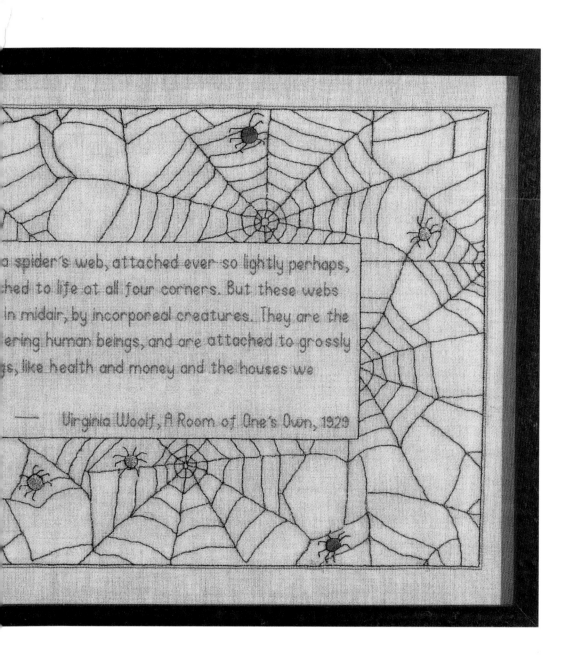

a spider's web, attached ever so lightly perhaps,
...hed to life at all four corners. But these webs
...in midair, by incorporeal creatures. They are the
...ering human beings, and are attached to grossly
...gs, like health and money and the houses we

— Virginia Woolf, A Room of One's Own, 1929

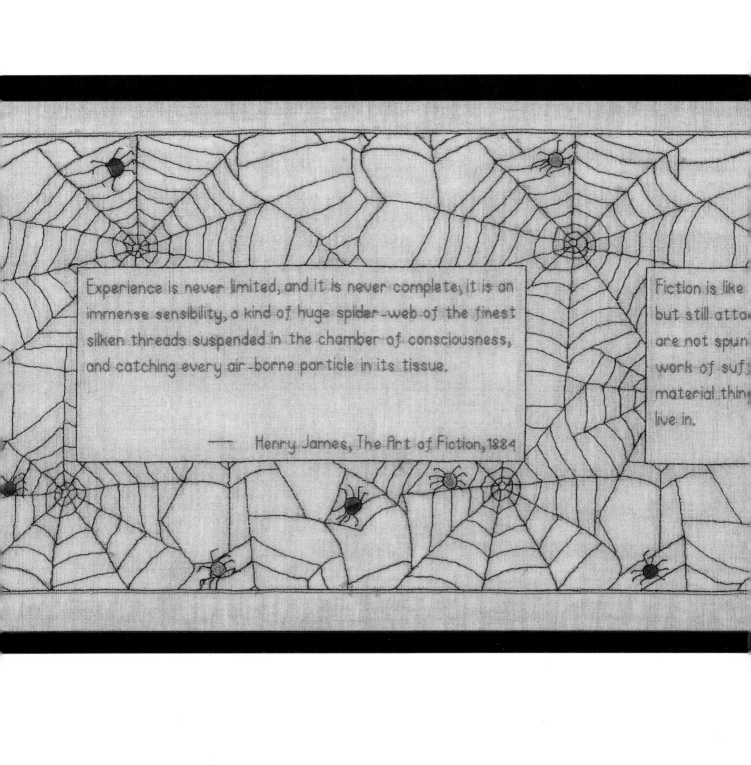

Experience is never limited, and it is never complete; it is an immense sensibility, a kind of huge spider-web of the finest silken threads suspended in the chamber of consciousness, and catching every air-borne particle in its tissue.

—— Henry James, The Art of Fiction, 1884

Fiction is like
but still atta
are not spun
work of suf
material thing
live in.

8. Sampler (Hercules)

THE STORY IS TOLD, IN OVID'S *HEROIDES* AMONG OTHER places, that when the Greek hero Hercules committed a murder the gods punished him by giving him as a slave to the queen of Lydia, Omphale, for a period of three years. He fell in love with her, they wore each other's clothes, and he spent his time with all her maids spinning thread for her. His wife, Deianira, got wind of this. He had abandoned her, had been unfaithful to her, but the thing that really got her mad was the damage this story did to his reputation. So she wrote him a letter. I quote Ovid's version of it.

Ernest Thesiger was an actor in post–World War I London who took his needlepoint with him wherever he went, apparently to the horror of British society. He also wrote a book called *Adventures in Embroidery*. Actually Thesiger had fought on the front during the war, and he tried to start an embroidery program for shell-shocked war veterans. Rosey Grier was a different kind of combat veteran, a professional football player, and, like Thesiger, he enjoyed doing needlepoint enough to write a book about it: *Rosey Grier's Needlepoint for Men.*

Hercules, when you touch the basket of wool does not your mighty hand cringe?

Ovid [43B.C.–17 A.D.], Heroides

Nothing is more terrifying to me than to see Ernest Thesiger sitting under the lamplight doing his embroidery.

Beverley Nichols, in The Sketch, London, 1929

It seems that needlepoint is as old as time.... Try it once, you'll keep on coming back for more!

Rosey Grier, Rosey Grier's Needlepoint for Men, 1973

Ernest Thesiger

Hercules and Omphale

Rosey Grier

9. Sampler (The Ultimate)

MODERNISM HAD ALL THESE IDEAS OF THE ABSOLUTE, THE ultimate, the goal beyond which no further advance would be possible. The Bauhaus school was advanced in many ways, but it suffered the burdens of this particular kind of idealism: it favored geometry and absolutes, which are implicitly rigid and inorganic.

I borrowed the border of this sampler from a design by Anni Albers, who taught weaving at the Bauhaus. It's geometric and gridded—the longer bars are all three times the length of the shorter ones. Anni Albers was the wife of Josef Albers, also a teacher at the school, who made square paintings. Georg Muche, also of the Bauhaus, is basically saying, men think, women do. Adolf Loos is from an older generation that left its mark on the Bauhaus. He wrote a notorious book called *Ornament and Crime* in which he associates women with the decorative and ornamental, and describes the ornamental as distinctly terrible.

So this sampler is based on geometry, but on geometry gone wild. I contained the design within a square frame, but made it crowded and ornate and gave it lush ornamental color. The interior is natural and organic as opposed to geometric—butterflies, flowers, urns that I see as anthropomorphic. A single flower escapes from the square at the top. There's also a mirroring going on, and for me this kind of doubling always suggests statement and counterstatement, ego and alter ego, a shadow world in which everything is the same but different. One butterfly flies up, the other down, but they're the same butterfly.

THE ULTIMATE OF BAUHAUS IDEALS: THE INDIVIDUAL SQUARE.
TALENT IS A SQUARE, GENIUS AN ABSOLUTE SQUARE.
— paul westheim, critic, 1923

THE FUNDAMENTAL CHARACTERISTIC OF FEMALE
CREATIVITY IS...ORNAMENTAL LIVELINESS.
— hans hildebrandt, art historian, 1928

ORNAMENT IS SOMETHING THAT MUST BE
OVERCOME.
— adolf loos, architect, 1898

IN THE HANDS OF THE WOMEN WEAVERS, MY ALPHABET OF
FORMS FOR ABSTRACT PAINTINGS TURNED INTO FANTASY....
I PROMISED MYSELF THAT I WOULD NEVER...WITH MY OWN
HANDS WEAVE A SINGLE THREAD.
— georg muche, form master, bauhaus weaving workshop

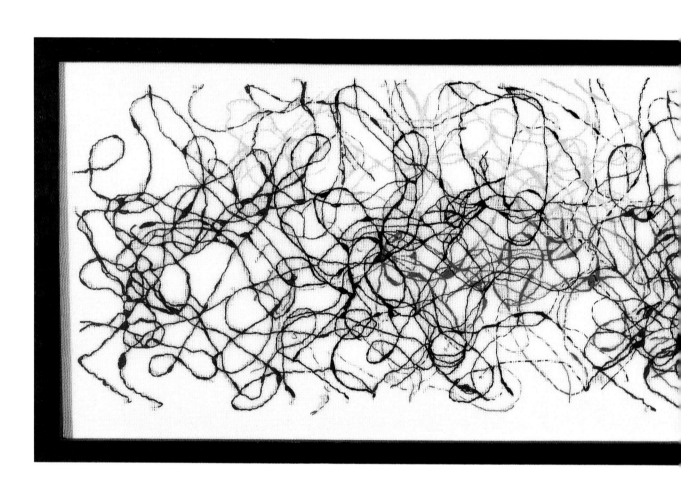

10. *Sampler (Andy Warhol)*

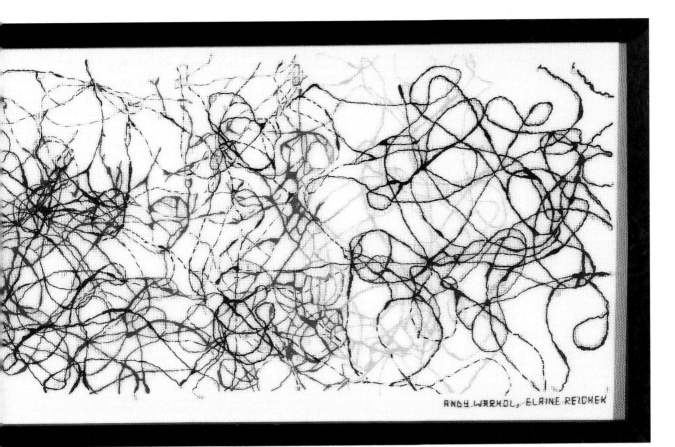

11. Sampler (Chuck Close)

WHEN CHUCK CLOSE BEGAN MAKING HIS WELL-KNOWN images of heads, in the late 1960s, portraiture was definitely outré—in fact, painting itself was mistakenly thought to have died. But by working on a very large scale, by inventing weird kinds of verisimilitude, and by devising an ingenious range of methods (this particular image, a self-portrait, was made by amalgamating countless wads of different-colored paper), Close revitalized the genre.

I think one of the things that appealed to him about taking on this job was simply the idea of attempting to do something that no one thought a serious artist could do any more. It's like Robert Scott and the South Pole: you say it can't be done? I'll do it! And I'll do it really big! The funny thing is, though, that a process that seemed so unconventional was actually what women had always done in needlepoint. Close bases his works on a grid—he breaks the image down into tiny squares, then fills in each square one by one, until together they reconstitute the image. Embroidery, likewise, rests on the grid of a woven textile, and in cross-stitch you're basically filling in an image square by square. I've seen drawings by Close that show how he plots the image as a kind of graph or chart—which is exactly what I often do before making a sampler.

CHUCK CLOSE, ELAINE REICHEK

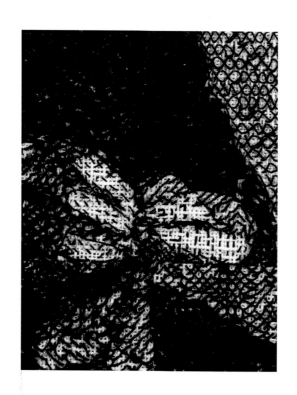

12. *Sampler (Georges Seurat)*

13. Sampler (Kruger/Holzer)

THE ALPHABET SAMPLER WAS A LEARNING TOOL, A PEDA-gogical device used to teach girls their sewing and their letters at the same time. For *Sampler (Kruger/Holzer)* I combined two different examples, both band samplers (that means the design is based on tiers of horizontal rows), and set them side by side. They're both from New England and were produced within a dozen years of each other—they're similar designs.

The original embroiderers were Hannah Breed in 1756 and Phebe Smith in 1768. You had to be skilled to make one of these samplers; at age nine, Hannah Breed used a whole vocabulary of different stitches—cross, long-arm cross, eyelet, florentine, herringbone, lazy daisy, rococo, satin, and straight. Most of those appeared in patterns and figures that I omitted. Since I was only doing the letters, I used mainly cross-stitch.

Besides removing the decorative patterns, I added extra alphabets to the original designs and adjusted the colors and the proportions. I also added the maxims; the originals just had the letters of the alphabet. I used the kind of sayings that often appear in samplers as well as phrases with a similar instructional tone from the works of the contemporary artists Barbara Kruger and Jenny Holzer. Samplers like these, with their lines of moral dicta listed one above the other, always remind me of the Ten Commandments.

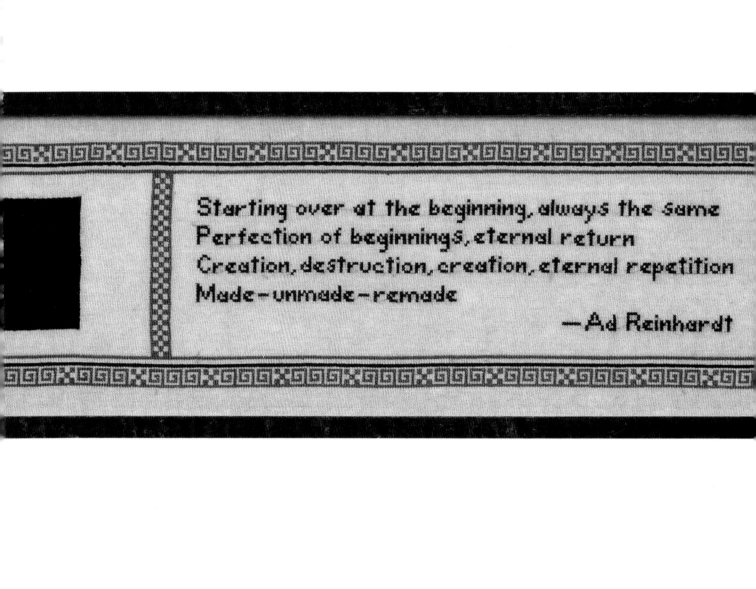

Starting over at the beginning, always the same
Perfection of beginnings, eternal return
Creation, destruction, creation, eternal repetition
Made – unmade – remade

—Ad Reinhardt

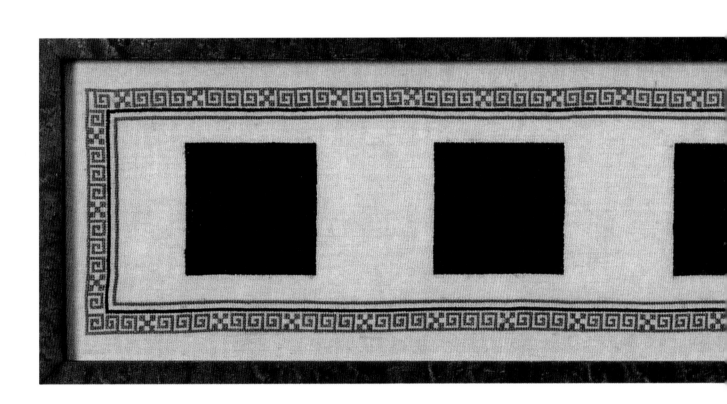

15. *Sampler (Anon.)*

For this sampler I appropriated an early-nineteenth-century design, a sampler that's a multiplication table. I was drawn to its allover grid, which is both rigorous and childishly simple, and I liked the inflections that the shape of each number gives to each of the boxes. I also liked the repetition that brings progress—you keep doing the same thing, in little steps, and eventually you get to where you're going, to 12 x 12 = 144. The idea that little steps taken in sequence add up to something struck me as resembling the repetition of stitches—each stitch is a tiny mark, but the overall accretion ends up as a pattern or picture. So this icon of learning step by step by step, additively, is very much like embroidery.

The only difference between my sampler and the original is the two signatures. The original just says "Multiplication Table" on top; I added "Anon. 1825" to the left and my own initials and "1998" to the right.

I wound my schemes on my distaff
I would weave that mighty web by day
But then by night, by torchlight
I undid what I had done

—Penelope, The Odyssey

14. *Sampler (Starting Over)*

READING FROM LEFT TO RIGHT, I REVERSED THE ORDINARY chronological sequence in this sampler by putting the modern artist Ad Reinhardt on the left and Penelope and ancient Greece on the right. That allowed me to end on the right with a design from a Greek vase, which would have originally been circular; so built into the sampler is a doubling back and circling around. Ad was my teacher at art school, which makes this sampler quite personal for me, but I could have chosen a number of artists for a quote like his here—Piet Mondrian, Sol LeWitt, and others have said similar things, emphasizing process rather than result. In a way, I'm setting up Penelope as the first process artist.

For me a gridded painting, like Ad's or like Mondrian's, is a magnification of its support, since the weave of linen or canvas is a grid. The three squares on the left are adaptations of the paintings by Ad that at first look solid black but have a barely visible grid of color. The border in the sampler is also based on a grid—the ancient Greek key design, which appears in classical architecture and is a series of square modules. I interpolated the little cross—it's the design of Ad's painting in another form.

Once when I was a student I went to Ad's Manhattan studio, which was on Broadway. I went up the stairs. The door was open; he didn't hear me come in. I saw him silhouetted against the big Broadway windows. He was sanding down the edge between the squares in one of these gridded paintings to make sure there was no trace of a line where they abutted—that the paint flowed seamlessly and that color was the only differential. That extreme attention to detail was so impressive about him. A line between the squares would have changed the meaning of the painting.

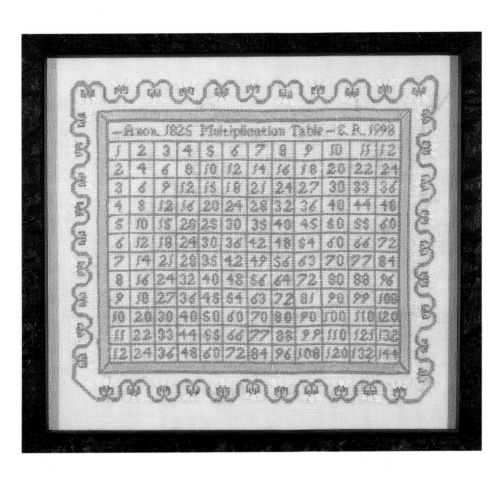

– Anon. 1825   Multiplication Table – C. R. 1998

1	2	3	4	5	6	7	8	9	10	11	12
2	4	6	8	10	12	14	16	18	20	22	24
3	6	9	12	15	18	21	24	27	30	33	36
4	8	12	16	20	24	28	32	36	40	44	48
5	10	15	20	25	30	35	40	45	50	55	60
6	12	18	24	30	36	42	48	54	60	66	72
7	14	21	28	35	42	49	56	63	70	77	84
8	16	24	32	40	48	56	64	72	80	88	96
9	18	27	36	45	54	63	72	81	90	99	108
10	20	30	40	50	60	70	80	90	100	110	120
11	22	33	44	55	66	77	88	99	110	121	132
12	24	36	48	60	72	84	96	108	120	132	144

16. Sampler (Jasper Johns)

I AM STRUCK BY HOW MUCH JASPER JOHNS'S WHITE *Numbers* of 1958 looks like the multiplication sampler that I examined in *Sampler (Anon.)*.

In works like *White Numbers* Johns uses a stencil to lay down a regular pattern, then paints over it. The surface is an accretion of many tiny strokes to make a field, and the field doesn't necessarily follow the underlying pattern of the stencil. The work depends on the tension between the sensitivity of Johns's touch and the stencil's regularized, programmed form.

To me, the way Johns lays down his brushstrokes relates to the way stitches are laid down. That overlay of the hand on a regular pattern is the stitching process. With stitches you can't vary the pressure of your touch the way you can with a brush, but you can work the individual strands for nuance and get just as interesting a surface—by bunching, spacing, using different stitches. You use the stitches that produce the configuration you want.

Samplers are sometimes classed as Americana, which is also linked to Johns. The 1950s paintings with three-dimensional elements look as if he'd been scouring junk shops for folk art. And then there are the flag paintings, which, supposedly, are based on a design made in sewing by Betsy Ross.

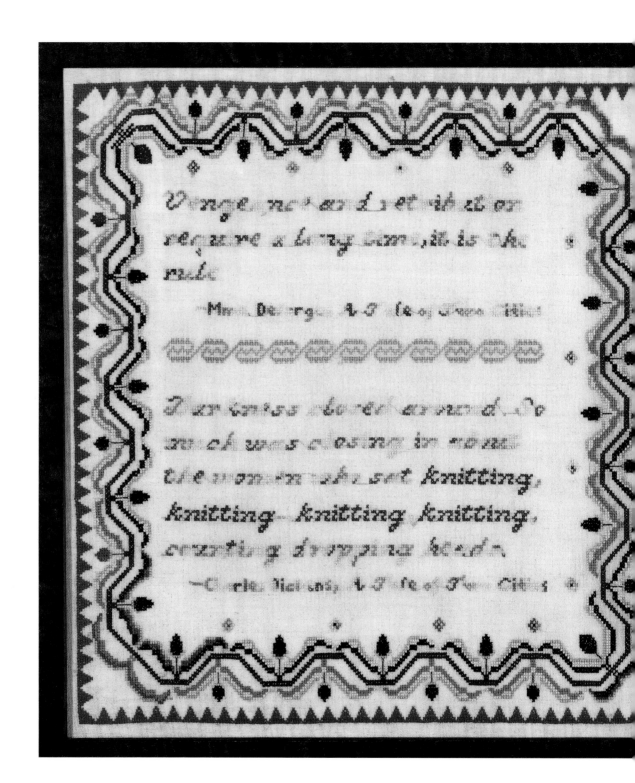

17. *Sampler (Vengeance)*

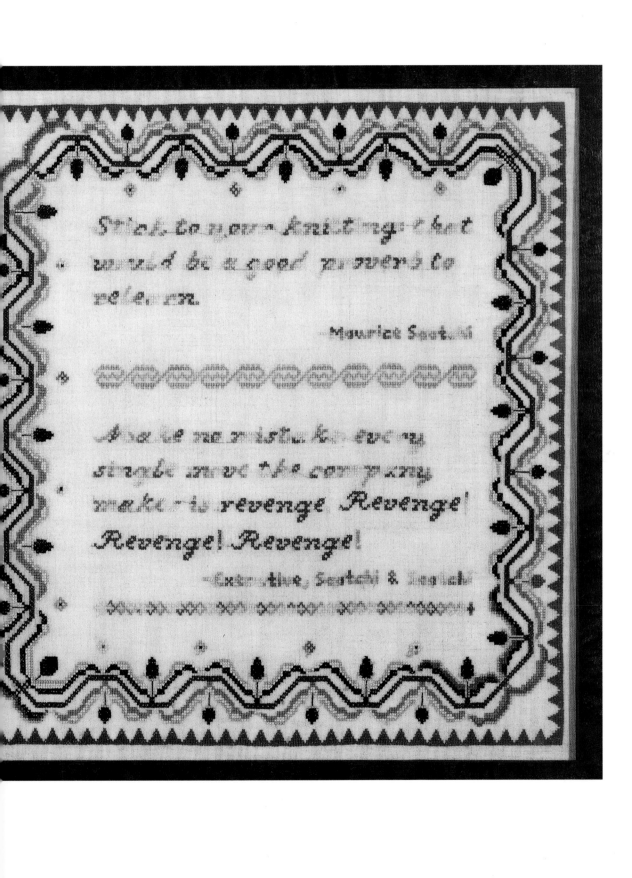

Stick to your knitting; that would be a good proverb to relearn.

—Maurice Saatchi

Make no mistake every single move the company makes is revenge Revenge! Revenge! Revenge!

—Executive, Saatchi & Saatchi

18. *Sampler (Dispositional Hypnoid States)*

CLEARLY FREUD HAD A LOW OPINION OF NEEDLEWORK, but all the women in his family did handicrafts of one kind or another. In fact, there's a letter in which Freud warns his daughter Anna that her constant knitting will ruin her eyes and posture. Anna wove as well; her loom is still in the family's house in Hampstead, London, which is now the Freud Museum. She became a psychoanalyst herself, of course, and the story goes that she used to knit through her patients' sessions (as Colette might say, maybe she was thinking). It amused me to pair the quote from Colette, about a woman's silence while sewing, with a quote from the man who invented the talking cure.

The sampler design I based this piece on had more motifs—a house, trees, a vase—which I removed to make space for the text. It's eighteenth-century American, so it really has nothing to do with either Freud or Colette. But the motifs around the border, which are actually florals, have little antennae and seem to metamorphose into insects—a creepy effect out of Kafka that may have led me to Central Europe and to Freud.

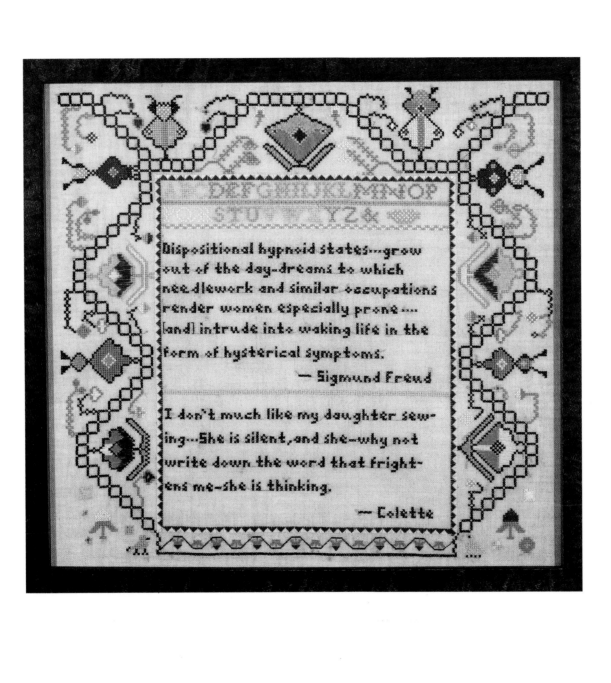

ABCDEFGHIJKLMNOP
STUVWXYZ&

Dispositional hypnoid states...grow
out of the day-dreams to which
needlework and similar occupations
render women especially prone ...
[and] intrude into waking life in the
form of hysterical symptoms.
— Sigmund Freud

I don't much like my daughter sewing...She is silent, and she—why not
write down the word that frightens me—she is thinking.

— Colette

19. *Sampler (Mary Queen of Scots)*

Imprisoned in the Tower of London by her cousin Elizabeth, Mary Queen of Scots passed the time making embroideries (now in the Victoria & Albert Museum). I printed the picture of her by phototransferring a contemporary portrait onto satin, which I sewed into the sampler. It's like a miniature, a little keepsake.

Chidiock Tichborne was a supporter of Mary's who was involved in a plot to free her from the Tower. He got caught and wrote this poem while awaiting execution. As far as I know, it is the only poem of his that survives, and it is extraordinarily sophisticated. It is so odd and yet so correct that his string of Beckett-like paradoxes echoes Mary's own motto, which is quoted below: "In my end is my Beginning."

It seems to me that the circularity of the motto and of the poem is also embedded in the sampler. It's seventeenth century—a little later than Mary's time but pretty much in the same style—and the S's in the sampler stand for "Stuart," Mary's surname. The horizontal bands in band samplers like this one are details of larger patterns; you can see how the pattern would repeat, but it's not fully developed. The sides of these truncated patterns are left open, to tell you that they could be extended indefinitely. So they imply infinity—they have no end—but at the same time the pattern is cut, interrupted, like Tichborne's thread that is simultaneously cut and not yet spun. Also, the pattern at the top is repeated again at the bottom, but at the top it's multicolored and at the bottom it's gone gray. The central motif is an interlocking chain.

My youth is gone, and yet I am but
young;
I saw the world and yet I was not
seen;
My thread is cut, and yet it is not
spun;
And now I live and now my life is done.
— Chidiock Tichborne

In my end is   my Beginning.

— Mary Queen of Scots

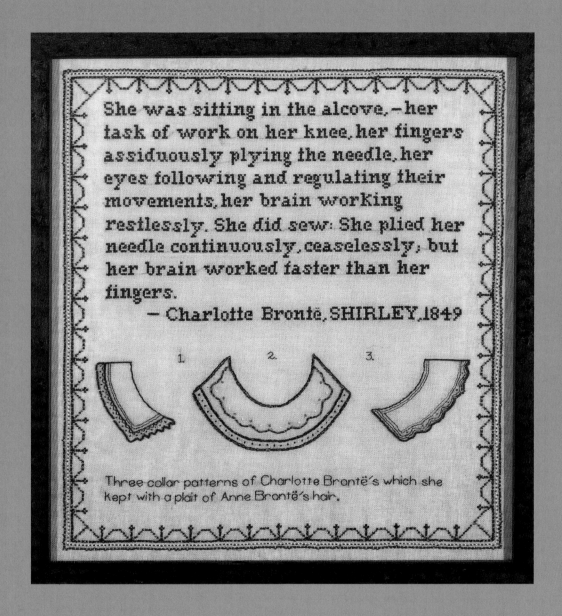

She was sitting in the alcove,—her
task of work on her knee, her fingers
assiduously plying the needle, her
eyes following and regulating their
movements, her brain working
restlessly. She did sew: She plied her
needle continuously, ceaselessly; but
her brain worked faster than her
fingers.
— Charlotte Brontë, SHIRLEY, 1849

1.　　　　2.　　　　3.

Three collar patterns of Charlotte Brontë's which she
kept with a plait of Anne Brontë's hair.

20. *Sampler (The Brontës—She Was Sitting),* part 1 of 5

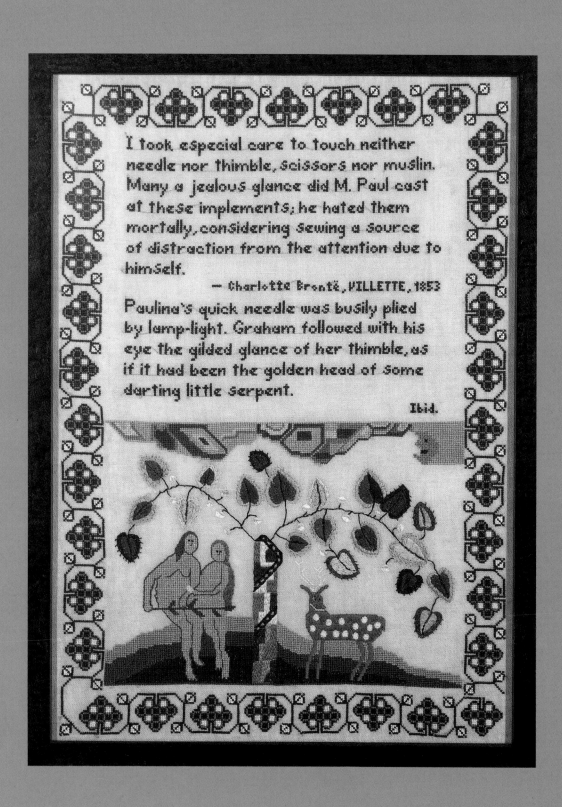

I took especial care to touch neither needle nor thimble, scissors nor muslin. Many a jealous glance did M. Paul cast at these implements; he hated them mortally, considering sewing a source of distraction from the attention due to himself.

— Charlotte Brontë, VILLETTE, 1853

Paulina's quick needle was busily plied by lamp-light. Graham followed with his eye the gilded glance of her thimble, as if it had been the golden head of some darting little serpent.

Ibid.

21. *Sampler (The Brontës—I Took Especial Care),* part 2 of 5

22. *Sampler (The Brontës—Emily Jane Brontë)*, part 3 of 5

23. *Sampler (The Brontës—I Am Pleased)*, part 4 of 5

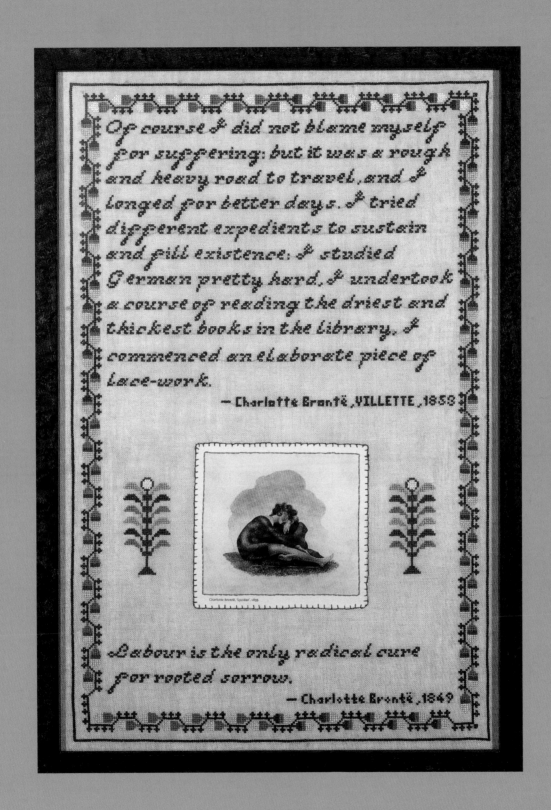

Of course I did not blame myself for suffering; but it was a rough and heavy road to travel, and I longed for better days. I tried different expedients to sustain and fill existence: I studied German pretty hard, I undertook a course of reading the driest and thickest books in the library, I commenced an elaborate piece of lace-work.

— Charlotte Brontë, VILLETTE, 1853

Charlotte Brontë, "Lycidas", 1835

Labour is the only radical cure for rooted sorrow.

— Charlotte Brontë, 1849

24. *Sampler (The Brontës—Of Course)*, part 5 of 5

25. Sampler (Silhouette)

THIS IS THE KIND OF IMAGE YOU OFTEN SEE AS A MASS-produced print or a paper cutout in the hall or guest bathroom of a suburban house—it has no particular meaning, and it's nothing people value enough to put anywhere they'd really look at it. But I think showing it as an embroidery in the context of *When This You See...* makes you read it in a different way.

The man sits below the woman and has to look up to her. He is winding wool for her, which is a passive role—a couple of pegs would serve just as well—and she is busy and focused; he is lending himself to her project. I guess he is active in a way, in that he is clearly her suitor, but all the power seems to lie with her. I mean, his hands are tied. It's a peculiar thing—he temporarily gives up the dominance you would expect him to want to maintain in the pitching-woo relationship and hands it over to her. And it is her work in wool that sanctions this.

Images like this one derive from the nineteenth-century silhouette tradition, but you do sometimes see them in embroideries. I took this particular example from a book published by the Center for the History of American Needlework. The motif is commonplace; I have an old print, I think a nineteenth-century book illustration, that expresses the same idea.

The Lady of Shalott

There she weaves by night and day
A magic web with colors gay.

She knows not what the curse may be,
And so she weaveth steadily,

But in her web she still delights,
To weave the mirror's magic sights.

26. Sampler (Tennyson)

The three printed images in this sampler are copies of paintings from around the turn of the twentieth century by J. W. Waterhouse, who did a series of works based on Alfred, Lord Tennyson's poem "The Lady of Shalott." The Lady looks different in each painting (different decades, different models), but they're all her. The A. S. Byatt quote comes from *The Conjugial Angel*, a novella of 1992 in which one character is Tennyson's ghost. Since Byatt likens Tennyson to a nightingale, I embroidered some of those birds darting around the linen. The nightingale for me, of course, is Philomela, subject of *Sampler (Ovid's Weavers)*.

In the poem, the Lady of Shalott lives in a tower. She is under a curse that forbids her from looking outside—she doesn't know what the consequence might be, but she sees the outdoors only as it is reflected in a mirror, and spends her nights and days weaving. Then one day the knight Lancelot rides by. She sees him in the mirror, goes to the window, and looks out. The curse falls and she shortly dies. The poem seems to be a parable of art and of sexuality: you can look at life through art—in an image—but if you look at it directly, or if you admit your desire for it, it will kill you. I don't believe that, but I do recognize the solitude that Tennyson describes, the isolation of making art.

In Tennyson's poetry the Lady of Shalott is the prototype for a character in his later work *Idylls of the King*—another woman in Lancelot's love life, the "lily maid of Astolat," whose name is Elaine.

afraid–terribly afraid–
...ns of overvaluing
...what came to him
...ously; he knew the
...ork wildly without a
...a aim, singing away like
...le.

A.S. Byatt, The Conjugial Angel, 1992

She left the web, she left the loom,
She made three paces thro' the room,
. . . .
   She look'd down to Camelot.
Out flew the web and floated wide;
The mirror crack'd from side to side;
"The curse is come upon me," cried
   The Lady of Shalott.

                    Alfred, Lord Tennyson, 1842

Tennyson was
of the temptatio
Art. Art was
easily and fur
temptation to u
conscience or a
the Nightinga

27. Sampler (Doily)

SINCE SO MANY WOMEN HAVE MADE EMBROIDERIES AND other handworks that are left unsigned—these anonymous labors that end up in thrift shops and rummage sales—I wanted to include something made by someone else besides me. So I bought a doily in a thrift shop, then literally took it apart and put it back together again. I reconstructed its meaning, both physically and metaphorically; I wanted to serve someone else's work, someone else's meaning, while also combining them with my own.

The quote, from the Irish novelist Edna O'Brien, describes a contrary piece of crocheting in which "a piece of straight thread was converted into a tight and unrippable little conundrum." I imagined this conundrum as a tight, impenetrable little knot—the Gordian knot on another scale—and a doily is full of tiny knots. It also seemed to me that I had knotted the original meaning together with mine, so that they can't be untangled. Finally, O'Brien's novel, *Down by the River*, is about the knotty, seamy issues of incest and abortion, the latter, particularly in Ireland, being as dangerous a topic as the former. It's a contemporary story, but for me it resonates with Greek myth—Philomela raped by her brother-in-law; O'Brien's character Mary a schoolgirl raped by her father.

She would sit +
and watch the crochet
needle loop forward then
quickly backward then forward
again so that a piece of straight
thread was converted into a
+ tight and unrippable little
conundrum. - - - - - - - - - -
—Edna O'Brien, Down by
the River, 1997 +

28. Sampler (Kierkegaard's Handkerchief)

I BOUGHT THE WHITE HANDKERCHIEF JUST THE WAY I bought the doily for *Sampler (Doily)*. Then I embroidered my name and the spider's web and stuck in the pins. The quote in the other panel comes from "The Seducer's Diary," which Søren Kierkegaard published as fiction but is thought to be highly autobiographical. It's part of a bigger book called *Either/Or*.

The scene is a flirtation, obviously, but who is the hunter and who is the prey? Who is looking at whom? Who has trapped the other? The couple are playing this game, and in church, of all places. The pins aren't sewing pins, they're specimen pins—the kind you'd pin a butterfly with. They're long and black and they pierce.

There's a tension in Kierkegaard's book between eros and the rigor of the writer's mind. So I kept the color austere—that northern thought, a sense of chill—but the shape of the handkerchief is subtly anthropomorphic and feminine, and its folds imply secrecy, something hidden inside. I've used the two-panel format many times, but in this particular case it reminds me of a book, and the handkerchief is like a flower pressed between its pages, that old custom. At the same time, it goes back in the other direction in its purity—it's like a nun's habit and wimple.

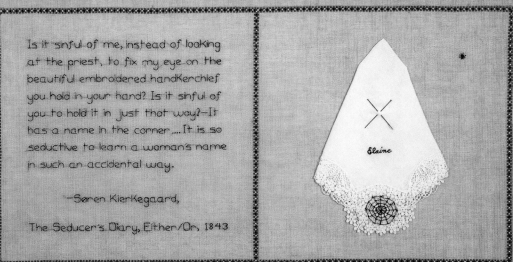

Is it sinful of me, instead of looking at the priest, to fix my eye on the beautiful embroidered handkerchief you hold in your hand? Is it sinful of you to hold it in just that way?—It has a name in the corner....It is so seductive to learn a woman's name in such an accidental way.

—Søren Kierkegaard,

The Seducer's Diary, Either/Or, 1843

Elaine

29. Sampler (World Wide Web)

I'm ALWAYS COMING ACROSS WORDS AND PHRASES THAT use the language of weaving and cloth—it suffuses our consciousness as a deeply embedded metaphor. We even talk about the fabric of life. And this metaphor runs right up through the most up-to-date technology.

In fact, there are links between the history of weaving and the computer. The jacquard loom, invented in the eighteenth century, is often considered an early example of a programmable machine—the prototype for that kind of thinking. Also, although the computer is considered a boy toy, in the early nineteenth century it was a woman, Ada Lovelace—the daughter of the poet Byron—who developed the mathematics and worked to refine a calculating machine, the Analytical Engine, devised by Charles Babbage. He provided the idea, she provided the system, the logic.

The pixel and the byte are like stitches—tiny indissoluble elements that in combination with thousands of other indissoluble elements make up a picture. Are there bugs in your computer? Maybe they're spiders.

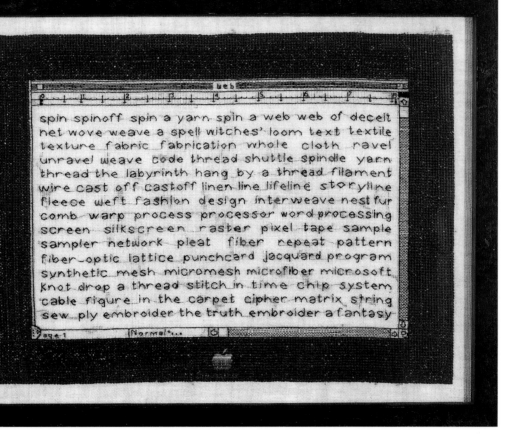

spin spinoff spin a yarn spin a web web of deceit
net wove weave a spell witches' loom text textile
texture fabric fabrication whole cloth ravel
unravel weave code thread shuttle spindle yarn
thread the labyrinth hang by a thread filament
wire cast off castoff linen line lifeline storyline
fleece weft fashion design interweave nest fur
comb warp process processor word processing
screen silkscreen raster pixel tape sample
sampler network pleat fiber repeat pattern
fiber-optic lattice punchcard jacquard program
synthetic mesh micromesh microfiber microsoft
knot drop a thread stitch in time chip system
cable figure in the carpet cipher matrix string
sew ply embroider the truth embroider a fantasy

30. Sampler (White on White)

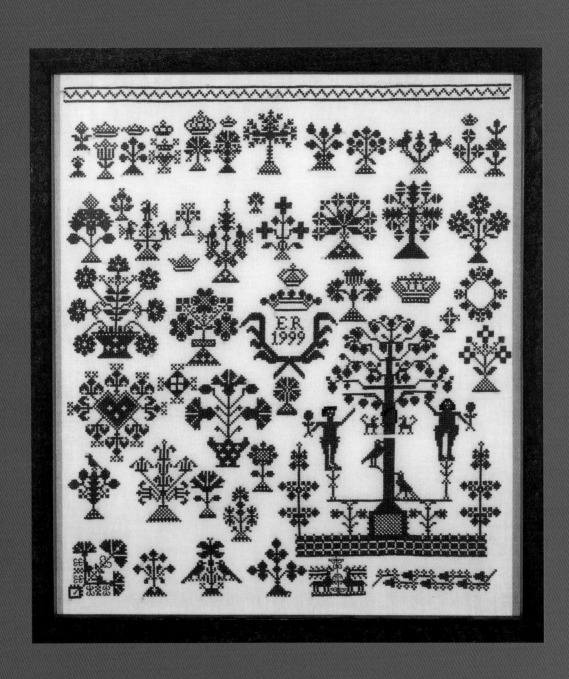

31. Sampler (Spot Sampler)

PLATES AND SOURCES

The texts that are quoted in the samplers appear below, along with their sources.

1. SAMPLER (OVID'S WEAVERS), 1996
Embroidery on linen, 19¼ x 35 in. (49.5 x 88.9 cm).
Collection of Melva Bucksbaum.

This embroidery is based on an American Quaker sampler made by Sarah Siddal in 1818.

> Arachne was renowned—but certainly not for her birthplace or her family. Yet consummate work had won the girl much fame. She weaves her pliant golden threads into her web—and traces some old tale.

From Ovid's *Metamorphoses*, trans. A. D. Melville, World Classics (New York: Oxford University Press, 1987).

> What shall Philomela do? Desperation can invent, in misery the mind is keen. She hangs a web upon a crude loom and, on a white background, weaves purple signs: the letters that denounce the savage crime.

From *The Metamorphoses of Ovid*, trans. Allen Mandelbaum (San Diego, New York, and London: Harcourt, Brace and Co., 1993).

2. SAMPLER (THE SCARLET LETTER), 1996
Embroidery on linen, 26½ x 12⅛ in. (66 x 30.8 cm).
Collection of Alexandra Bowes, San Francisco.

> SHE HATH GOOD SKILL AT HER NEEDLE...
> This rag of scarlet cloth assumed the shape of a letter. It was the capital letter A....Each limb proved to be precisely three inches and a quarter in length.
>
> The SCARLET LETTER, so fantastically embroidered and illuminated upon her bosom, had the effect of a spell, taking her out of the ordinary relations with humanity and enclosing her in a sphere by herself.
> —NATHANIEL HAWTHORNE

From Nathaniel Hawthorne's *The Scarlet Letter*, 1850 (New York: Airmont Books, 1962).

3. SAMPLER (MOBY DICK), 1997
Embroidery and twine on linen, 17½ x 13½ in. (44.5 x 34.3 cm). Collection of Melva Bucksbaum.

The original sampler was sewn in New England, around 1780.

> MOBY DICK
> A Sailor's Yarn
>
> ...Thus we were weaving and weaving away...
>
> I kept passing the woof of marline between the long yarns of the warp, using my own hand for the shuttle ...weaving away at the Fates
>
> ...God's foot upon the treadle of the loom...

From Herman Melville's *Moby Dick*, 1851 (Boston: Houghton Mifflin Co., 1956).

4. SAMPLER (IT WAS SOMETHING), 1998
Embroidery on linen, 21¼ x 27¾ in. (54.6 x 70.5 cm).
Collection of Melva Bucksbaum.

> It was something, I guessed, in the primal plan; something like a complex figure in a Persian carpet.... to trace the figure in the carpet through every convolution, to

reproduce it in every tint…would be the
greatest literary portrait ever painted.

> Henry James, The Figure In The Carpet

From Henry James's "The Figure in the Carpet," 1896, in
James, *The Figure in the Carpet and Other Stories* (London:
Penguin Books, 1986).

5. SAMPLER (THE SECRET CODE), 1997
Embroidery on linen, 8¼ x 21½ in. (21 x 54.6 cm).
Collection of Melva Bucksbaum.

The left side of the sampler is embroidered with the alpha-
betical code invented by Potter and used in her diaries. See
*The Journals of Beatrix Potter, 1881–1887, Transcribed from
Her Code Writings by Leslie Linder* (London: Frederick
Warne, 1966).

> Three little mice sat down to spin,
> Pussy passed by and she peeped in.
> What are you at, my fine little men?
> Making coats for gentlemen.
> Shall I come in and cut off your threads?
> Oh, no, Miss Pussy, you'd bite off our heads!
>
> The Tailor Of Gloucester, by Beatrix Potter

From Beatrix Potter's *The Tailor of Gloucester* (London: F.
Warne and Co., 1903).

6. SAMPLER (THE LITTLE WORK-TABLES),
1996
Embroidery on linen, 19 x 19¼ in. (48.3 x 48.9 cm).
Collection of Stephanie Farber, Branford, Connecticut.

This work is based on an American sampler by Martha
Smith, completed in 1809.

> THE LITTLE WORK-TABLES OF WOMEN'S FINGERS,
> ARE THE PLAYGROUND OF WOMEN'S FANCIES, AND
> THEIR KNITTING-NEEDLES ARE THE FAIRY-WANDS
> BY WHICH THEY TRANSFORM A WHOLE ROOM
> INTO
> A SPIRIT ISLE OF DREAMS.
>
> —JENNY JUNE

Jenny June [Jane Croly], in an 1885 issue of *Knitting and
Crochet*.

> Knit 2, Purl 1,
> Hubby 0.
> —Ogden Nash

Ogden Nash, quoted in *The Saturday Evening Post*, April 1982.

7. SAMPLER (A SPIDER), 1997
Embroidery on linen, 14½ x 49¼ in. (36.8 x 114.9 cm).
Collection of Melva Bucksbaum.

> A spider darted forth four or five threads from its
> spinners.
> Glittering in the sunshine, a film of silk blown by the
> wind, these
> diverged in an ascending direction. The spider then let
> go its
> hold, and was quickly borne from sight. The
> atmosphere can
> never be so tranquil, as not to affect a vane so delicate
> as the
> thread of a spider's web.
> —Charles Darwin, Aeronaut Spiders, 1833

From Charles Darwin's *Journal of Researches into the Geology
and Natural History of the Various Countries Visited by H.M.S.
Beagle by Charles Darwin*. A facsimile reprint of the first
edition, 1839 (New York and London: Hafner Publishing
Co., 1952).

> Experience is never limited, and it is never complete, it
> is an
> immense sensibility, a kind of huge spider-web of the
> finest
> silken threads suspended in the chamber of
> consciousness,
> and catching every air-borne particle in its tissue.
> —Henry James, The Art of Fiction, 1884

From Henry James's "The Art of Fiction," 1884, in James,
The Critical Muse: Selected Literary Criticism (London:
Penguin Books, 1987).

> Fiction is like a spider's web, attached ever so lightly
> perhaps,
> but still attached to life at all four corners. But these webs
> are not spun in midair, by incorporeal creatures. They
> are the
> work of suffering human beings, and are attached to
> grossly
> material things, like health and money and the houses
> we live in.
> —Virginia Woolf, A Room of One's Own, 1929

From Virginia Woolf's *A Room of One's Own* (San Diego,
New York, and London: Harcourt Brace Jovanovich,
1929).

8. SAMPLER (HERCULES), 1997
Embroidery on linen, 22 x 17¼ in. (55.9 x 45.1 cm).
Collection of Melva Bucksbaum.

> Hercules, when you touch the basket of wool does not
> your mighty hand cringe?
> > Ovid [43 B.C.–17 A.D.], Heroides

From Deianira's letter to her husband, Hercules, in Ovid's
Heroïdes, trans. Harold Isbell (London: Penguin Books,
1993).

> Nothing is more terrifying to me than to see
> Ernest Thesiger sitting under the lamplight
> doing his embroidery.
> > Beverley Nichols, in The Sketch, London, 1929

Beverly Nichols in *The Sketch* (London, 1929).

> It seems that needlepoint is as old as time.... Try it
> once, you'll keep on coming back for more!
> Rosey Grier, Rosey Grier's Needlepoint for Men, 1973

From *Rosey Grier's Needlepoint for Men* (New York: Walker
and Co., 1973).

9. SAMPLER (THE ULTIMATE), 1996
Embroidery on linen, 21¼ x 21¼ in. (54 x 54 cm).
Collection of Melva Bucksbaum.

The border design was copied from a weaving motif by
Anni Albers.

> THE ULTIMATE OF BAUHAUS IDEALS: THE
> INDIVIDUAL SQUARE.
> TALENT IS A SQUARE, GENIUS AN ABSOLUTE
> SQUARE.
> > —paul westheim, critic, 1923

From Paul Westheim's "Comments on the 'Squaring' of the
Bauhaus," in *Das Kunstblatt*, vol. 7 (Potsdam, 1923).

> IN THE HANDS OF THE WOMEN WEAVERS, MY
> ALPHABET OF
> FORMS FOR ABSTRACT PAINTINGS TURNED
> INTO FANTASY....
> I PROMISED MYSELF THAT I WOULD NEVER...
> WITH MY OWN
> HANDS WEAVE A SINGLE THREAD.
> > —georg muche, form master, bauhaus weaving workshop

From Georg Muche's *Blickpunkt* (Tübingen: Verlag Ernst
Wasmuth, 1965).

> THE FUNDAMENTAL CHARACTERISTIC OF FEMALE
> CREATIVITY IS...ORNAMENTAL LIVELINESS.
> > —hans hildebrandt, art historian, 1928

From Hans Hildebrandt's *Die Frau als Kunstlerin* (Berlin:
Mosse Verlag, 1928).

> ORNAMENT IS SOMETHING THAT MUST BE
> OVERCOME.
> > —adolf loos, architect, 1898

From Adolf Loos's "Ladies Fashion," 1898, in *Spoken into the
Void: Collected Essays 1897–1900*, trans. Jane O. Newman
and John H. Smith (Cambridge, Mass.: The MIT Press,
1982).

10. SAMPLER (ANDY WARHOL), 1997
Embroidery on linen, 10¼ x 30¼ in. (26 x 78.1 cm).
Collection of Susan Unterberg, New York.

Copied from Andy Warhol, *Yarn*, 1983, synthetic polymer
and silk screen on canvas, 54 x 206 inches (1.37 x 5.23 m).

11. SAMPLER (CHUCK CLOSE), 1997
Embroidery on linen, 11 x 8½ in. (27.9 x 21.6 cm).
Collection of Allen W. Prusis, New York.

Copied from Chuck Close, *Self Portrait*, 1983, pulp paper on
canvas, 54 x 40 inches (1.37 x 1 m). Private collection.

12. SAMPLER (GEORGES SEURAT), 1998
Embroidery on linen, 13⅛ x 11⅝ in. (34 x 29.6 cm).
Collection of the artist.

Copied from Georges Seurat's *The Artist's Mother (Woman
Sewing)*, 1882–83, Conté crayon on paper, 12¼ x 9½ inches
(31.1 x 24.1 cm). Collection of The Metropolitan Museum
of Art, New York. Purchase, Joseph Pulitzer Bequest, 1955
(55.21.1).

13. SAMPLER (KRUGER/HOLZER), 1998
Embroidery on linen, 30½ x 21¼ in. (77.5 x 55.3 cm).
Collection of Melva Bucksbaum.

The embroidery on the left is based on a sampler made by
Phebe Smith in New England in 1768. Hannah Breed
stitched the other in 1756, when she was nine, in Lynn,
Massachusetts.

> A fool and his money
> are soon parted.
> Phebe Smith 1768

I shop therefore I am.
Barbara Kruger, 1987

From Barbara Kruger's *Untitled (I shop therefore I am)*, 1987, photographic silk screen/vinyl, 111 x 113 in. (2.82 x 2.87 m).

DO AS YOU WOULD BE DONE BY.
Hannah Breed 1756

ABUSE OF POWER COMES AS NO SURPRISE. JENNY HOLZER, 1977

From Jenny Holzer, untitled, 1977, offset poster on paper, street installation, Manhattan, New York.

14. SAMPLER (STARTING OVER), 1996
Embroidery on linen, 8¼ x 67½ in. (22.2 x 171.4 cm). Collection of The Museum of Modern Art, New York. Marcia Riklis Fund. Photograph: Thomas Powel, New York.

The embroidery copies, on the left, three paintings by Ad Reinhardt, and on the right, a design from a Greek vase (c. 560 B.C.) showing women engaged in textile work.

Starting over at the beginning, always the same
Perfection of beginnings, eternal return
Creation, destruction, creation, eternal repetition
Made—unmade—remade
—Ad Reinhardt

From Ad Reinhardt's *Art As Art: The Selected Writings of Ad Reinhardt*, ed. Barbara Rose, The Documents of Twentieth-Century Art (New York: Viking Press, 1975).

I wound my schemes on my distaff
I would weave that mighty web by day
But then by night, by torchlight
I undid what I had done
—Penelope, The Odyssey

Penelope in *The Odyssey of Homer*, trans. Richard Lattimore (New York: Harper Collins, 1965).

15. SAMPLER (ANON.), 1998
Embroidery on linen, 9½ x 10½ in. (25.3 x 26.7 cm). Collection of Wellesley College, Gift of Jacqueline L. Fowler, Wellesley, Massachusetts.

Based on an American miniature multiplication-table sampler sewn around 1825.

16. SAMPLER (JASPER JOHNS), 1997
Embroidery on linen, 12¼ x 11 in. (32.4 x 27.9 cm). Collection of Ellen Celli, New York.

Copied from Jasper Johns, *White Numbers*, 1958, encaustic on canvas, 28 x 22 inches (71.1 x 55.9 cm). Collection of David Geffen, Los Angeles.

17. SAMPLER (VENGEANCE), 1996
Embroidery on linen, 19¼ x 33¼ in. (49.5 x 85.7 cm). Private collection, New York.

Vengeance and retribution
require a long time, it is the
rule.
—Mme. Defarge, A Tale of Two Cities

Darkness closed around. So
much was closing in about
the women who sat knitting,
knitting...knitting, knitting,
counting dropping heads.
—Charles Dickens, A Tale of Two Cities

From Charles Dickens's *A Tale of Two Cities*, 1859 (U.S. and Canada: Bantam, 1983).

Stick to your knitting: that
would be a good proverb to
relearn.
—Maurice Saatchi

Maurice Saatchi, quoted in Steven Schiff's "Master of Illusion," *The New Yorker*, 15 May 1995. The quotation also appeared in Fiametta Rocco's "Saatchi's Revenge," *Vanity Fair*, June 1995.

Make no mistake: every
single move the company
makes is revenge. Revenge!
Revenge! Revenge!
—Executive, Saatchi & Saatchi

A Saatchi and Saatchi executive, quoted in Fiametta Rocco's "Saatchi's Revenge," *Vanity Fair*, June 1995.

18. SAMPLER (DISPOSITIONAL HYPNOID STATES), 1996
Embroidery on linen, 18¾ x 20¼ in. (47.6 x 51.4 cm). Collection of Melva Bucksbaum.

Dispositional hypnoid states...grow

out of the day-dreams to which
needlework and similar occupations
render women especially prone....
[and] intrude into waking life in the
form of hysterical symptoms.
—Sigmund Freud

From Sigmund Freud's preface to "Studies on Hysteria,
1883–1885," 1895, in S. Freud and J. Breuer, *The Complete
Psychological Works of Sigmund Freud*, vol. 2 (London: The
Hogarth Press, 1932–36).

I don't much like my daughter sewing... She is silent, and she—why not
write down the word that frightens me—she is thinking.
—Colette

From Colette's *Earthly Paradise* (London: Secker and
Warburg, 1966).

19. SAMPLER (MARY QUEEN OF SCOTS), 1996
Embroidery and transfer print on linen, 35¼ x 10¾ in.
(89.5 x 27.3 cm). Private collection, New York.

Based on a sampler by E. K., from 1653, in the collection of
the Fitzwilliam Museum, Cambridge, England.

My youth is gone, and yet I am but
young;
I saw the world and yet I was not
seen;
My thread is cut, and yet it is not
spun;
And now I live and now my life is done.
—Chidiock Tichborne

From Chidiock Tichborne's "Tichborne's Elegy" (1586),
Norton Anthology of Poetry, 3rd ed. (New York and London:
W. W. Norton and Co., 1983).

In my end is my Beginning.
—Mary Queen of Scots

Mary Queen of Scots, quoted in Antonia Fraser's *Mary
Queen of Scots* (London: Weidenfeld and Nicolson, 1969).

20. SAMPLER (THE BRONTËS—SHE WAS
SITTING), PART 1 OF 5, 1997
Embroidery and beading on linen, 17¼ x 16½ in. (43.8 x
41.9 cm). Collection of Andrew Solomon, New York, in
memory of Carolyn B. Solomon.

Based on three collar patterns embroidered by Charlotte
Brontë, which she kept with a plait of Anne Brontë's
hair. See Christine Alexander and Jane Sellars, *The Art
of the Brontës* (Cambridge: Cambridge University Press,
1995).

She was sitting in the alcove,—her
task of work on her knee, her fingers
assiduously plying the needle, her
eyes following and regulating their
movements, her brain working
rèstlessly. She did sew: She plied her
needle, continuously, ceaselessly, but
her brain worked faster than her
fingers.
—Charlotte Brontë, SHIRLEY, 1849

From Charlotte Brontë's *Shirley*, 1849 (New York: Oxford
University Press, 1981).

21. SAMPLER (THE BRONTËS—I TOOK
ESPECIAL CARE), PART 2 OF 5, 1997
Embroidery and beading on linen, 22⅛ x 16½ in.
(56.8 x 41.9 cm). Collection of Andrew Solomon, New
York, in memory of Carolyn B. Solomon.

The original sampler, by Ann Bowden, is believed to have
been sewn in 1811 in the north of England.

I took especial care to touch neither
needle nor thimble, scissors nor muslin.
Many a jealous glance did M. Paul cast
at these implements; he hated them
mortally, considering sewing a source
of distraction from the attention due to
himself.
—Charlotte Brontë, VILLETTE, 1853

Paulina's quick needle was busily plied
by lamp-light. Graham followed with his
eye the gilded glance of her thimble, as
if it had been the golden head of some
darting little serpent.
Ibid.

From Charlotte Brontë's *Villette*, 1853 (London: Penguin,
1987).

22. SAMPLER (THE BRONTËS—EMILY JANE
BRONTË), PART 3 OF 5, 1997
Embroidery on linen, 9¼ x 11 in. (23.5 x 27.9 cm).

Collection of Andrew Solomon, New York, in memory of Carolyn B. Solomon.

Copied from a sampler made by Emily Brontë in 1828. The original is in the collection of the Haworth Parsonage, Yorkshire, once the home of the Brontë family.

23. SAMPLER (THE BRONTËS—I AM PLEASED), PART 4 OF 5, 1997

Embroidery and beading on linen, 10⅜ x 14¼ in. (26.4 x 36.2 cm). Collection of Andrew Solomon, New York, in memory of Carolyn B. Solomon.

The motif was copied from the same sampler by Ann Bowden adapted for *The Brontës—I Took Especial Care* (plate 21).

> I am pleased that you cannot quite decide whether I am\of the soft or the hard sex/an attorney's clerk or a novel-reading dress-maker.... I had better bind myself apprentice to a chemist & druggist if I am a young gentleman or to a Mantua maker & milliner if I am a young lady....
> Charlotte Brontë, 1840

Charlotte Brontë in a letter of 1840 to her publishers, quoted in Janet Barker's *The Brontës* (New York: St. Martin's Press, 1994).

24. SAMPLER (THE BRONTËS—OF COURSE), PART 5 OF 5, 1997

Embroidery and transfer print on linen, 22¼ x 15½ in. (56.5 x 39.4 cm). Collection of Andrew Solomon, New York, in memory of Carolyn B. Solomon.

The satin insert is printed from a sketch by Charlotte Brontë, dated 1855. See Christine Alexander and Jane Sellars, *The Art of the Brontës* (Cambridge: Cambridge University Press, 1995).

> Of course I did not blame myself for suffering: but it was a rough and heavy road to travel, and I longed for better days. I tried different expedients to sustain and fill existence: I studied German pretty hard, I undertook a course of reading the driest and thickest books in the library, I commenced an elaborate piece of lace-work.
> —Charlotte Brontë, VILLETTE, 1853

From Charlotte Brontë's *Villette*, 1853 (London: Penguin, 1987).

> Labour is the only radical cure for rooted sorrow.
> —Charlotte Brontë, 1849

Charlotte Brontë in a letter of 1849 to William Smith Williams, quoted in Janet Barker's *The Brontës* (New York: St. Martin's Press, 1994).

25. SAMPLER (SILHOUETTE), 1998

Embroidery on linen, 8½ x 9¾ in. (47 x 24.8 cm). Private collection, New York.

Copied from one of the samplers in *Ann Orr's Charted Designs* (New York: The Center for the History of American Needlework and Dover Publications, Inc., 1978).

26. SAMPLER (TENNYSON), 1998

Embroidery and transfer print on linen, 18⅜ x 45 in. (46.7 x 114.3 cm). Collection of Melva Bucksbaum.

> The Lady of Shalott
>
> There she weaves by night and day
> A magic web with colors gay.
> . . . .
> She knows not what the curse may be,
> And so she weaveth steadily,
> . . . .
> But in her web she still delights,
> To weave the mirror's magic sights,
> . . . .
> She left the web, she left the loom,
> She made three paces thro' the room,
> . . . .
> She look'd down to Camelot.
> Out flew the web and floated wide;
> The mirror crack'd from side to side;
> "The curse is come upon me," cried
> The Lady of Shalott.
> Alfred, Lord Tennyson, 1842

From Alfred, Lord Tennyson's "The Lady of Shalott," 1842, in *Tennyson's Poetry*, ed. Robert W. Hill, Jr. (New York and London: W. W. Norton and Co., 1971).

> Tennyson was afraid—terribly afraid—
> of the temptations of overvaluing
> Art. Art was what came to him

easily and furiously; he knew the
temptation to work wildly without a
conscience or an aim, singing away like
the Nightingale.

A. S. Byatt, The Conjugial Angel, 1992

From A. S. Byatt's "The Conjugial Angel," 1992, in *Angels and Insects* (New York: Random House, Inc., 1994).

The three images, printed on satin, are copies of paintings by J. W. Waterhouse:

'I am Half sick of Shadows', said The Lady of Shalott, 1916, oil on canvas, 39½ x 29 in. (100.5 x 73.7 cm). Art Gallery of Ontario, Toronto.

The Lady of Shalott, 1894, oil on canvas, 56 x 34 in. (142.2 x 86.4 cm). Leeds City Art Gallery.

The Lady of Shalott, 1888, oil on canvas, 60½ x 78¼ in. (1.5 x 2 m). Tate Gallery, London.

27. SAMPLER (DOILY), 1998
Embroidery on linen, 20¼ x 20¼ in. (51.4 x 51.4 cm). Private collection, New York.

> She would sit
> and watch the crochet
> needle loop forward then
> quickly backward then forward
> again so that a piece of straight
> thread was converted into a
> tight and unrippable little
> conundrum.
> —Edna O'Brien, Down by
> the River, 1997

From Edna O'Brien's *Down by the River* (New York: Farrar, Straus and Giroux, 1997).

28. SAMPLER (KIERKEGAARD'S HANDKERCHIEF), 1998
Specimen pins and embroidery on linen, 12½ x 22½ in. (31.8 x 57.2 cm). Private collection, Los Angeles.

> Is it sinful of me, instead of looking
> at the priest, to fix my eye on the
> beautiful embroidered handkerchief
> you hold in your hand? Is it sinful of
> you to hold it in just that way?—It
> has a name in the corner....It is so

seductive to learn a woman's name
in such an accidental way.
—Søren Kierkegaard,
The Seducer's Diary, Either/Or, 1843

From Søren Kierkegaard's "The Seducer's Diary," in *Either/Or*, 1843 (Princeton, N. J.: Princeton University Press, 1997).

29. SAMPLER (WORLD WIDE WEB), 1998
Embroidery on linen, 11¼ x 14¼ in. (28.6 x 36.2 cm). Collection of Allen W. Prusis, New York.

> spin spinoff spin a yarn spin a web web of deceit
> net wove weave a spell witches' loom text textile
> texture fabric fabrication whole cloth ravel
> unravel weave code thread shuttle spindle yarn
> thread the labyrinth hang by a thread filament
> wire cast off castoff linen line lifeline storyline
> fleece weft fashion design interweave nest fur
> comb warp process processor word processing
> screen silkscreen raster pixel tape sample
> sampler network pleat fiber repeat pattern
> fiber-optic lattice punchcard jacquard program
> synthetic mesh micromesh microfiber microsoft
> knot drop a thread stitch in time chip system
> cable figure in the carpet cipher matrix string
> sew ply embroider the truth embroider a fantasy

A free association of words plotted on an Apple laptop screen.

30. SAMPLER (WHITE ON WHITE), 1999
Embroidery on linen, 18¼ x 16¼ in. (46.4 x 41.3 cm). Courtesy Nicole Klagsbrun Gallery, New York.

The patterns were copied from two seventeenth-century English band samplers.

31. SAMPLER (SPOT SAMPLER), 1999
Embroidery on linen, 18¼ x 16¼ in. (46.4 x 41.3 cm). Courtesy Nicole Klagsbrun Gallery, New York.

Copied from a sampler stitched by A. W. in 1756 in Vierlande, Germany.

Unless noted otherwise, the photographs are by Adam Reich.

SELECTED EXHIBITIONS AND BIBLIOGRAPHY

Elaine Reichek was born and lives in New York, N.Y.

SELECTED SOLO EXHIBITIONS

1978   Parsons Dreyfuss Gallery, New York, N.Y.

1979   Parsons Dreyfuss Gallery, New York, N.Y.
        Special Projects: Artist's Bedroom, Institute for Art and Urban Resources, P.S. 1, Long Island City, N.Y.

1980   Lois I. Clifford Gallery, Pittsburgh Center for the Arts, Pittsburgh, Pa.
        Douglass College Art Gallery, Walters Hall, New Brunswick, N.J.
        Brownson Art Gallery, Manhattanville College, Purchase, N.Y.

1981   A.I.R. Gallery, New York, N.Y.

1982   Concord Gallery, New York, N.Y.

1985   *Houses*, Snug Harbor Museum, Staten Island, N.Y. (with Vito Acconci and Ira Joel Haber)
        Center on Contemporary Art, Seattle, Wash.
        A.I.R. Gallery, New York, N.Y.

1986   *Investigations, 19: Elaine Reichek*, Institute of Contemporary Art, University of Pennsylvania, Philadelphia, Pa.

1987   Philadelphia College of Art and Design, Philadelphia, Pa.
        Transfigurations, Carlo Lamagna Gallery, New York, N.Y.
        Photocollages, Carlo Lamagna Gallery, New York, N.Y.
        A.I.R. Gallery, New York, N.Y. (with Patsy Norvell)

1988   *Desert Song*, Barbara Braathen Gallery, New York, N.Y.
        Revenge of the Coconuts: A Curiosity Room, 56 Bleecker Street Gallery, New York, N.Y.

1989   *Fatal Passage*, Everson Museum of Art, Syracuse, N.Y.
        Visitations, Carlo Lamagna Gallery, New York, N.Y.

1990   Braunstein Quay Gallery, San Francisco, Calif.
        The War Room, Carlo Lamagna Gallery, New York, N.Y.

1992   *Elaine Reichek: Tierra del Fuego*, Akron Art Museum, Akron, Ohio
        Elaine Reichek: Native Intelligence, Grey Art Gallery, New York University, New York, N.Y.; Greenville
            County Museum of Art, Greenville, S.C.; Cleveland Center for Contemporary Art, Cleveland, Ohio;
            Western Gallery, Western Washington State University, Bellingham, Wash.

1993   *Home Rule*, Irish Museum of Modern Art, Dublin, Ireland; Orchard Gallery, Derry, Northern Ireland
        Sign Language, Norton Gallery of Art, West Palm Beach, Fla.

1994   *A Postcolonial Kinderhood*, The Jewish Museum, New York, N.Y.; Jewish Museum, San Francisco, Calif.;
        Wexner Center for the Visual Arts, Columbus, Ohio
        Model Homes, Stichting De Appel, Amsterdam, Holland
        At Home in America, Center for Research in Contemporary Art, University of Texas, Arlington, Tex.

1995   *Form Security Administration*, Michael Klein Gallery, New York, N.Y.

1996   *Guests of the Nation*, Rosenwald-Wolf Gallery, University of the Arts, Philadelphia, Pa.; Van
        Every/Smith Galleries, Davidson College, Davidson, N.C.

1999   *Projects 67: Elaine Reichek*, The Museum of Modern Art, New York, N.Y.
        Nicole Klagsbrun Gallery, New York, N.Y.

2000   Palais des Beaux-Arts, Brussels, Belgium

SELECTED GROUP EXHIBITIONS

1978   *Ten Cases on Eighth Avenue*, Artists Space in conjunction with New York City Department of
        Transportation, New York, N.Y.
        Visions: Paper/Multiples, Diane Gilson Gallery, Seattle, Wash.
        Out of the House, Whitney Museum of American Art, Downtown at Federal Plaza, New York, N.Y.
        New York Collection, Albright-Knox Art Gallery, Buffalo, N.Y.

1979   *Illusions in Clay, Fiber, Glass, Metal, Wood and Plastics*, Summit Art Center, Summit, N.J.
        Small Is Beautiful, Freedman Gallery, Albright College, Reading, Pa.

1980   *Structure, Narrative, Decoration*, McIntosh Drysdale Gallery, Washington, D.C.
        U.S.A. Women Artists, Museo de Arte Contemporanea, São Paulo, Brazil
        System, Inquiry, Translation, Touchstone Gallery, New York, N.Y.

1981   Lund Konsthalle, Lund, Sweden
        Home Work: The Domestic Environment Reflected in the Work of Contemporary Women Artists, National
        Women's Hall, Seneca Falls, N.Y.; Joe and Emily Lowe Art Gallery, Syracuse University, Syracuse,
        N.Y.; Henry Street Settlement, New York, N.Y.; Amelie A. Wallace Gallery, State University of New
        York at Old Westbury, Old Westbury, N.Y.
        Contemporary Artists, Henry Street Settlement, New York, N.Y.; and tour

1982   Concord Gallery, New York, N.Y.
        Women Sculptors' Drawings, Max Hutchinson Gallery, New York, N.Y.

1983   *Fauna: The Animal Ally*, Lehman College, Bronx, N.Y.
        C.A.P.S. Fellowships Recipients Graphics Exhibition, F.I.T. Gallery, New York, N.Y.
        Walls of the Seventies, QCC Gallery, Queensborough Community College, Bayside, N.Y.
        Day in, Day Out, Freedman Gallery, Albright College, Reading, Pa.

1984   *Ecstasy*, Monique Knowlton Gallery, New York, N.Y.
        Neue Stofflichkeit, Frauen Museum, Bonn, West Germany

1985   *New York Art Now: Correspondences*, La Forêt Museum, Tokyo, Japan; Tochigi Prefectural Museum of
        Fine Arts, Tochigi, Japan; Tazaki Hall Espace Media, Kobe, Japan
        Connections, Leila Taghiana-Milani Gallery, New York, N.Y.

1986   *Traps: Elements of Psychic Seduction*, Carlo Lamagna Gallery, New York, N.Y.

Connections, Three Rivers Arts Festival, Pittsburgh, Pa.
Let's Play House, Bernice Steinbaum Gallery, New York, N.Y.

1987   *Art on Paper*, Weatherspoon Art Gallery, University of North Carolina, Greensboro, N.C.
Third Inaugural Exhibition, Carlo Lamagna Gallery, New York, N.Y.
A New York State Invitational, Rice Gallery, Albany, N.Y.

1988   *Dwellings*, 56 Bleecker Gallery, New York, N.Y.
Sixth International Triennale of Tapestry, Łódź, Poland
Just Like a Woman, Greenville County Museum of Art, Greenville, S.C.
Frontiers in Fiber: The Americans, North Dakota Museum of Art, Grand Forks, N.D.; Metropolitan
    Museum of Art, Manila, Philippines; Hong Kong Art Center, Hong Kong; National Art Gallery,
    Singapore

1989   *The Big Picture*, Rena Bransten Gallery, San Francisco, Calif.
Photocollage/Photomontage: The Changing Picture, 1920–89, Jan Turner Gallery, Los Angeles, Calif.
Explorations, Staller Center Art Gallery, State University of New York, Stony Brook, N.Y.

1990   *Landscape/Mindscape*, Carlo Lamagna Gallery, New York, N.Y.
Cultural Artifacts, Ehlers Caudill Gallery, Chicago, Ill.
Exoticism, Ezra and Cecile Zilkha Gallery, Wesleyan University, Middletown, Conn.
The New School Collects: Recent Acquisitions, New School for Social Research, New York, N.Y.

1991   *American Art Today: New Directions*, Art Museum, Florida International University, Miami, Fla.
Site Seeing: Travel and Tourism in Contemporary Art, Whitney Museum of American Art,
    Downtown at Federal Plaza, New York, N.Y.
Totem, Boca Raton Museum of Art, Boca Raton, Fla.
Inherent Vice, Center for Photography, Woodstock, N.Y.
The Subversive Stitch, Simon Watson, New York, N.Y.
The Interrupted Life, New Museum of Contemporary Art, New York, N.Y.
Burning in Hell, Franklin Furnace, New York, N.Y.
Constructing Images: Synapse between Photography and Sculpture, Lieberman & Saul Gallery, New
    York, N.Y.; Tampa Museum of Art, Tampa, Fla.; Center for Creative Photography, University of
    Arizona, Tucson, Ariz.; San Jose Museum of Art, San Jose, Calif.
Constructions of Meaning, University Galleries, Illinois State University, Normal, Ill.

1992   *Dark Decor*, De Pree Art Center, Hope College, Holland, Mich.; San Jose Museum of Art, San
    Jose, Calif.; Florida Gulf Coast Art Center, Belleair, Fla.
Imaging Indians, Longwood Arts Gallery, Bronx, N.Y.
Specs, Annina Nosei Gallery, New York, N.Y.
Winter's Edge, Okun Gallery, Santa Fe, N.M.

1993   *American Art Today: Clothing as Metaphor*, Art Museum, Florida International University, Miami, Fla.
Contacts Proofs, Jersey City Museum, Jersey City, N.J.
The Empty Dress, Neuberger Museum, State University of New York, Purchase, N.Y.; Virginia Beach
    Center for the Arts, Virginia Beach, Va; University Art Gallery, University of North Texas, Denton,
    Tex.; Art Gallery, University of Newfoundland, Nova Scotia, Canada; Mackenzie Art Gallery, Regina,
    Saskatchewan, Canada; Gallery Stratford, Stratford, Ontario, Canada; Weatherspoon Art Gallery,
    University of North Carolina, Greensboro, N.C.; Selby Gallery, Ringling School of Art and Design,
    Sarasota, Fla.; Montclair Art Museum, Montclair, N.J.; Schafler Gallery, Pratt Institute, Brooklyn, N.Y.
U.S.A. Today, Nederlands Textielmuseum, Tilburg, Holland; Konstindustriemuseet, Helsinki, Finland

Myths and Legends as Told and Retold, Barbara Krakow Gallery, Boston, Mass.

Spoleto Festival, Spoleto, Italy

Ciphers of Identity, Fine Arts Gallery, University of Maryland/Baltimore County, Catonsville, Md.; Ronald Feldman Fine Arts, New York, N.Y.

Kurswechsel, Michael Klein, Inc., at Transart Exhibitions, Cologne, Germany

Addressing the Body, Terrain Gallery, San Francisco, Calif.; Patricia Shea Gallery, Santa Monica, Calif.

The Return of the Cadavre Exquis, Drawing Center, New York, N.Y.; and tour

The Figure as Fiction, Contemporary Arts Center, Cincinnati, Ohio

1994   *The Reading Room: Consider the Lilies*, Ruskin School of Art, Oxford University, Oxford, England

From Beyond the Pale, Irish Museum of Modern Art, Dublin, Ireland

Localities of Desire: Contemporary Art in an International World, Museum of Contemporary Art, Sydney, Australia

The Social Fabric, Beaver College Art Gallery, Glenside, Pa.

1995   *Division of Labor: Women's Work in Contemporary Art*, Bronx Museum of the Arts, Bronx, N.Y.; Los Angeles County Museum of Art, Los Angeles, Calif.

Conceptual Textiles: Material Meanings, John Michael Kohler Arts Center, Sheboygan, Wis.

A Print Extravaganza, Montclair Art Museum, Montclair, N.J.

Kunst Kabinett, Center on Contemporary Art, Seattle, Wash.

Laughter Ten Years After, Cecile and Ezra Zilkha Gallery, Wesleyan University, Middletown, Conn.; Beaver College Art Gallery, Glenside, Pa.

Photoworks from the Collection, Irish Museum of Modern Art, Dublin, Ireland

Art on Paper, Weatherspoon Art Gallery, University of North Carolina, Greensboro, N.C.

Thread Bare: Revealing Content in Contemporary Fiber, Southeastern Center for Contemporary Art, Winston-Salem, N.C.

Creation/Recreation, Islip Art Museum, East Islip, N.Y.

Zimmerdenkmäler, Museum Bochum, Bochum, Germany

1996   *Too Jewish*, The Jewish Museum, New York, N.Y.; Jewish Museum, San Francisco, Calif.; Armand Hammer Museum, University of California, Los Angeles, Calif.; Jewish Museum of Maryland, Baltimore, Md.

Labor of Love, New Museum of Contemporary Art, New York, N.Y.

Model Home, P.S. 1, The Clocktower, New York, N.Y.

Scratch, Thread Waxing Space, New York, N.Y.

Embedded Metaphor, John and Mable Ringling Museum of Art, Sarasota, Fla.; Western Gallery, Western Washington State University, Bellingham, Wash.; Bowdoin College Museum of Art, Bowdoin College, Brunswick, Me.; Contemporary Art Center of Virginia, Virginia Beach, Va.; Cecile and Ezra Zilkha Gallery, Wesleyan University, Middletown, Conn.; Pittsburgh Center for the Arts, Pittsburgh, Pa.

Making Pictures: Women and Photography, 1975–Now, Nicole Klagsbrun Gallery, New York, N.Y.; Bernard Toale Gallery, Boston, Mass.

1997   *Art on the Edge of Fashion*, Arizona State University Art Museum, Arizona State University, Tempe, Ariz.; Cranbrook Art Museum, Bloomfield Hills, Mich.

Auto Portrait: The Calligraphy of Power, Exit Art, New York, N.Y.

Women Artists of the 1970s, Jan Abrams Fine Arts, New York, N.Y.

Hanging by a Thread, Hudson River Museum of Westchester, Yonkers, N.Y.

1998   *Dimensions of Native America: The Contact Zone*, Museum of Fine Arts, Florida State University, Tallahassee, Fla.; Appleton Museum of Art, Ocala, Fla.

25 Years of A.I.R., Kingsborough Community College, Art Gallery of the City University of New York, Brooklyn, N.Y.

Loose Threads, Serpentine Gallery, London, England

Ethno-Antics, Nordiska Museet, Stockholm, Sweden

1999   *Other Narratives*, Contemporary Arts Museum, Houston, Tex.

Referencing the Past: Six Contemporary Artists, Addison Gallery of American Art, Phillips Academy, Andover, Mass.

New Displays from the Collection, Irish Museum of Modern Art, Dublin, Ireland

Girlschool, Brenau University Galleries, Brenau University, Gainesville, Ga.

2000   *Likeness of Being: Contemporary Self-Portraits by Fifty Women Artists*, DC Moore Gallery, New York, N.Y.

Déjà-vu, Katonah Museum of Art, Katonah, N.Y.

SELECTED BIBLIOGRAPHY

1978   Marter, Joan. "Elaine Reichek." *Arts Magazine*, January 1978, p. 7.

Newland, Joe. *Visions: Paper/Multiples.* Exh. cat. Seattle: Diane Gilson Gallery, 1978.

Zimmer, William. "Out of the House." *Soho Weekly News*, 16 February 1978.

1979   Dallier, Aline. "La Couture et la broderie dans l'art contemporain." *Bulletin des Arts Plastiques*, October 1979.

Zeitlin, Marilyn. *Small Is Beautiful.* Exh. cat. Reading, Pa.: Freedman Gallery, Albright College, 1979.

1980   Apgar, Evelyn. *Elaine Reichek.* Exh. cat. New Brunswick, N.J.: Douglass College Art Gallery, Walters Hall, 1980.

Park, Glenna. *U.S.A. Women Artists.* Exh. cat. São Paulo, Brazil: Museo de Arte Contemporanea, 1980.

Perreault, John. "Old Wine, New Bottles, Bad Year." *Soho Weekly News*, 18 June 1980.

Rice, Shelley. "System/Inquiry/Translation." *Artforum*, September 1980, pp. 70–71.

Rickey, Carrie. "System/Inquiry/Translation." *Village Voice*, 23 June 1980.

Robins, Corinne. "Artists Who Think and Art That Talks." *New York Arts Journal*, April 1980, pp. 22–24.

Russell, John. "Art: Collective Paradoxes for the Summer Season." *New York Times*, 20 June 1980, p. C27.

Thompson, Mary Lee. *Elaine Reichek.* Exh. cat. Purchase, N.Y.: Brownson Art Gallery, Manhattanville College, 1980.

1981   Fleming, Lee. "Structure/Narrative/Decoration." *New Art Examiner*, January 1981.

Hammond, Harmony. *Home Work: The Domestic Environment Reflected in Work by Contemporary Women Artists.* Exh. cat. Seneca Falls, N.Y.: National Women's Hall, 1981.

Levin, Kim, and Ann Sargent Wooster. "Elaine Reichek." *Village Voice*, 4 February 1981.

Perreault, John. "Art Attacks." *Soho Weekly News*, 18 February 1981.

———. "Homespun." *Soho Weekly News*, 15 December 1981, p. 22.

Rice, Shelley. "Elaine Reichek, A.I.R. Gallery." *Artforum*, April 1981, pp. 71–72.

Robins, Corinne. "Verbal Image/Written Object: Connection as Meaning in the Work of Elaine Reichek." *Arts Magazine*, February 1981, pp. 95–97.

1982   Levin, Kim. "Elaine Reichek." *Village Voice*, 2 November 1982.

Robins, Corinne. *Women Sculptors' Drawings.* Exh. cat. New York: Max Hutchinson Gallery, 1982.

———. "Women Sculptors' Drawings." *Women's Art Journal*, Spring/Summer 1982, pp. 22–23.

1983   Brody, Jacqueline. "Multiples & Objects & Books." *Print Collectors' Newsletter*, January/February 1983, p. 220.

Levin, Kim. "Elaine Reichek." *Flash Art*, January/February 1983, p. 65.

Moufarrege, Nicolas A. "X Equals Zero, as in Tic-Tac-Toe." *Arts Magazine*, February 1983, pp. 116–21.

Ratcliff, Carter. *Day in, Day Out*. Exh. cat. Reading, Pa.: Freedman Gallery, Albright College, 1983.

Robins, Corinne. *Walls of the Seventies*. Exh. cat. Bayside, N.Y.: QCC Gallery, Queensborough Community College, 1983.

Wooster, Ann Sargent. "Elaine Reichek at Concord." *Art in America*, March 1983, pp. 161–62.

1984 Hansen, Britta, and Marion Helbing-Mucke. *Neue Stofflichkeit*. Exh. cat. Bonn, West Germany: Frauen Museum, 1984.

Moufarrege, Nicolas. *Ecstasy*. Exh. cat. New York: Monique Knowlton Gallery, 1984.

Robins, Corinne. *The Pluralist Era: American Art, 1968–1981*. New York: Harper & Row, 1984.

1985 Chambers, Karen S. "Exhibitions—New York: Elaine Reichek." *Craft International*, April/May/June 1985, p. 37.

Downey, Roger. "On Visual Arts: The Art of Politics and Propaganda." *Seattle Times*, 26 June 1985, pp. 1, 44.

Jones, Alan. *New York Art Now: Correspondences*. Exh. cat. Tokyo: La Forêt Museum, 1985.

Levin, Kim. "Gimme Shelter." *Village Voice*, 17 December 1985, p. 108.

———. "Hanging Ten" and "Elaine Reichek." *Village Voice*, 12 March 1985, p. 76.

Medvedow, Jill. *Nancy Spero and Elaine Reichek*. Exh. cat. Seattle: Seattle Center on Contemporary Art, 1985.

Phillips, Patricia C. "Elaine Reichek." *Artforum*, May 1985, p. 105.

1986 Bohn, Donald Chant. "Investigations 1986." *New Art Examiner*, October 1986.

Liebmann, Lisa. *Investigations 19: Elaine Reichek*. Exh. cat. Philadelphia: Institute of Contemporary Art, University of Pennsylvania, 1986.

Perreault, John. *Connections*. Exh. cat. Pittsburgh: Three Rivers Arts Festival, 1986.

Sozanski, Edward J. "I.C.A. Investigates 4 Artist's Work." *Philadelphia Inquirer*, 19 June 1986, p. 5C.

1987 Flam, Jack. "The Gallery." *Wall Street Journal*, 27 February 1987.

Handy, Ellen. "Elaine Reichek." *Arts Magazine*, May 1987.

Indiana, Gary. "Short Memory: Elaine Reichek's Aboriginal Images." *Village Voice*, 17 February 1987, p. 95.

Levin, Kim. "Elaine Reichek." *Village Voice*, 17 February 1987.

———. "Patsy Norvell/Elaine Reichek." *Village Voice*, 4 March 1987.

McEvilley, Thomas. "Marginalia." *Artforum*, December 1987, pp. 6–7.

Princenthal, Nancy. "Elaine Reichek at Carlo Lamagna and A.I.R." *Art in America*, July 1987, p. 129.

1988 Constantine, Mildred, and Laurel Reuter. *Frontiers in Fiber: The Americans*. Exh. cat. Grand Forks, N.D.: North Dakota Museum of Art, 1988.

Levin, Kim. "Elaine Reichek." *Village Voice*, 14 June 1988, p. 52.

Mahoney, Robert. "Aloha Forever." *New York Press*, 17 June 1988.

Muller, Cookie. "Art and About." *Details*, August 1988.

Styron, Tom. *Just Like a Woman*. Exh. cat. Greenville, N.C.: Greenville County Museum of Art, 1988.

1989 "Art." *The New Yorker*, 17 April 1989.

Adams, Brooks. "Elaine Reichek." *Art in America*, July 1989, p. 132.

Aziz, Anthony. "Playing with the Big Ones." *Artweek*, 3 June 1989.

Handy, Ellen. "Installations and History." *Arts Magazine*, February 1989, pp. 62–65.

Levin, Kim. "Elaine Reichek." *Village Voice*, 25 April 1989.

Mahoney, Robert. "Home Is Where the Heart Is." *New York Press*, 20 January 1989.

Miller, Charles V. "Domestic Science." *Artforum*, March 1989, cover, pp. 117–20.

Nahas, Dominique. *Elaine Reichek*. Exh. cat. Syracuse, N.Y.: Everson Museum of Art, 1989.

Smith, Roberta. "Galleries Paint a Brighter Picture for Women." *New York Times*, 14 April 1989, pp. C1, C29.

1990   Hapgood, Susan. "Elaine Reichek." *Art in America*, June 1990, pp. 176–77.
        Haus, Mary. "Elaine Reichek." *Art News*, September 1990.
        Morgan, Susan. "Colonialism." *Aperture*, Spring 1990, cover, pp. 26–31.
        Muschamp, Herbert. "Trading Places." *House & Garden*, May 1990.
        Solnit, Rebecca. "Postmodern Primitive." *Art Week*, 7 July 1990, pp. 15–16.
        Zimmer, William. "Perceptions of the Other." *New York Times*, 11 February 1990, p. 32.

1991   Durham, Jimmie. "Legal Aliens." In *The Hybrid State*. Exh. cat. New York: Exit Art, 1991.
        Goldberg, Vicki. "Context Is All—or Nothing." *New York Times*, 7 July 1991, pp. 25–26.
        Handy, Ellen. "Photography's History/History's Photography." *Photography Center Quarterly* 12, no. 3 (1991): 14–18.
        Heartney, Eleanor. *American Art Today: New Directions*. Exh. cat. Miami: Art Museum, Florida International University, 1991.
        Lee, Pamela. *Site Seeing: Travel and Tourism in Contemporary Art*. Exh. cat. New York: Whitney Museum of American Art, Downtown at Federal Plaza, 1991.
        Levy, Jan Heller, ed. *The Interrupted Life*. Exh. cat. New York: New Museum of Contemporary Art, 1991.
        Mahoney, Robert. "Inherent Vice." *Photography Center Quarterly* 12, no. 3 (1991): 4–12.
        Olalquiaga, Celeste. "Nature Morte." *Lapiz*, April 1991, pp. 36–45.
        Schaffner, Ingrid. *Constructing Images: Synapse between Photography and Sculpture*. Exh. cat. New York: Lieberman & Saul Gallery, 1991.
        Selby, Roger. *Totem*. Exh. cat. Boca Raton, Fla.: Boca Raton Museum of Art, 1991.
        Smith, Roberta. "The Subversive Stitch." *New York Times*, 12 July 1991, p. C23.
        Spooner, Peter F. *Constructions of Meaning*. Exh. cat. Normal, Ill.: University Galleries, Illinois State University, 1991.
        Squiers, Carol. "Special Effects." *Artforum*, May 1991, pp. 25–26.

1992   "Art." *The New Yorker*, 13 April 1992, p. 12.
        Avgikos, Jan. "Elaine Reichek, Grey Art Gallery." *Artforum*, September 1992, p. 96.
        Cirincione, Janine, and Tina Potter. *Dark Decor*. Exh. cat. New York: Independent Curators, Inc., 1992.
        Durham, Jimmy, and Thomas McEvilley. *Elaine Reichek: Native Intelligence*. Exh. cat. New York: Grey Art Gallery, New York University, 1992.
        Hagen, Charles. "How American Indians Are Seen by the Nation." *New York Times*, 8 May 1992, p. C24.
        Hess, Elizabeth. "Difficult Pleasures." *Village Voice*, 21 April 1992, p. 93.
        Isaak, Jo Anna. "Who's 'We,' White Man?" *Parkett* no. 34 (Fall 1992): 142–51.
        Olalquiaga, Celeste. *Megalopolis: Contemporary Cultural Sensibilities*. Minneapolis: University of Minnesota Press, 1992.
        Princenthal, Nancy. "Elaine Reichek's 'Native Intelligence.'" *Print Collectors' Newsletter*, July/August 1992, pp. 94–95.
        Reichek, Elaine. "Artist's Statement." Exh. guide. New York: Grey Art Gallery, New York University, 1992.
        ———. "Elaine Reichek." *Tema Celeste*, Fall 1992, p. 71.
        ———. "Red Delicious." *Aperture Magazine*, Fall 1992, p. 51.
        Tannenbaum, Barbara. *Elaine Reichek: Tierra del Fuego*. Exh. cat. Akron, Ohio: Akron Art Museum, 1992.

1993   Bell, Desmond. "Elaine Reichek: Irish Museum of Modern Art." *Circa*, Fall 1993.
        Berger, Maurice. *Ciphers of Identity*. Exh. cat. Catonsville, Md.: Fine Arts Gallery, University of Maryland/Baltimore County, 1993.

Berger, Maurice, and Mildred Constantine. *USA Today.* Exh. cat. Tilburg, Netherlands: Nederlands Textielmuseum, 1993.

"Elaine Reichek." *New York Magazine,* 1 February 1993.

Engel, Laura, and Elaine Reichek. "Commentary: Mother/Daughter Dresses." *Fiberarts,* November/December 1993, p. 9.

Felshin, Nina. *The Empty Dress.* Exh. cat. New York: Independent Curators, Inc., 1993.

Friedman, Ann. "Elaine Reichek." *New Art Examiner,* May 1993, p. 51.

King, Elaine. *The Figure as Fiction.* Exh. cat. Cincinnati, Ohio: Contemporary Arts Center, 1993.

Larson, Kay. *American Art Today: Clothing as Metaphor.* Exh. cat. Miami: Art Museum, Florida International University, 1993.

Lichtenstein, Therese. "An Interview with Elaine Reichek." *Journal of Contemporary Art,* Winter 1993, pp. 92–107.

Mensing, Margo. "Elaine Reichek: Native Intelligence." *Art Papers,* March 1993, pp. 55–56.

———. "Elaine Reichek: Reevaluating Native Intelligence." *Fiberarts,* September/October 1993, p. 32.

Moroney, Mic. "Manufactured Identities." *Irish Times,* 12 May 1993.

Silverthorne, Jeanne. *Home Rule.* Exh. cat. Dublin: Irish Museum of Modern Art, 1993.

Stigter, Bianca. "Politieke boodschappen in de textielkunst." *NRC Handelsblad,* 3 May 1993.

Van den Berk, Hans. "Moderne Amerikaanse textielkunst." *Tilburg Magazine,* March 1993, p. 33.

Viso, Olga. *Sign Language.* Exh. brochure. West Palm Beach, Fla.: Norton Gallery of Art, 1993.

1994   Aukeman, Anastasia. "Elaine Reichek, The Jewish Museum." *Art News,* Summer 1994, pp. 179–80.

Bhabha, Homi K. *Model Homes.* Exh. cat. Amsterdam: Stichting De Appel, 1994.

Broude, Norma, and Mary D. Garrard. *The Power of Feminist Art.* New York: Abrams, 1994.

Corrin, Lisa G. "Installing History." *Art Papers* 18, no. 5 (July/August 1994): 6–13.

Cotter, Holland. "Review/Art." *New York Times,* 24 June 1994, p. C14.

Depondt, Paul. "Couleur Locale: Troosteloosheid en Indianenbehang." *Volkskrant,* 22 April 1994.

From beyond the Pale. Exh. cat. Dublin: Irish Museum of Modern Art, 1994.

Glueck, Grace. "Consumerama's Seductive Styling: Postcolonial Kinderhood." *New York Observer,* 21 March 1994.

Levin, Kim. "Choices." *Village Voice,* 16 August 1994, p. 65.

Liebmann, Lisa. "A Fashion Gallery: Eight New York Artists Interpret the New York Fall Collections." *New York Times Magazine,* 18 September 1994, p. 76.

Mahoney, Robert. "Elaine Reichek: Assimilation in America." *Fiberarts,* September/October 1994, pp. 57, 61.

Morgan, Anne Barclay. "Elaine Reichek: Sign Language." *Art Papers,* July/August 1994, pp. 46–47.

Murphey, Bernice. *Localities of Desire: Contemporary Art in an International World.* Exh. cat. Sydney, Australia: Museum of Contemporary Art, 1994.

Pedersen, Victoria. "Gallery Go 'Round." *Paper Magazine,* May 1994.

Peeters, Mark. "Galerie: Absalon/Reichek." *NRC Handelsblad,* 15 April 1994.

Reichek, Elaine. *At Home in America.* Exh. brochure. Arlington, Tex.: Center for Research in Contemporary Art, University of Texas at Arlington, 1994.

"Samplers of Jewish History." *Daily News* (New York), 4 February 1994.

Schwabsky, Barry. "Elaine Reichek: Jewish Museum." *Artforum,* October 1994, p. 104.

Slesin, Suzanne. "Perils of a Nice Jewish Girl in a Colonial Bedroom." *New York Times,* 17 February 1994, pp. C1, C6.

Weinberg, Helen. "An American Artist Samples Assimilation." *Forward,* 15 April 1994.

Whittemore, Emily. "Postcolonial Kinderhood." Exh. brochure. New York: The Jewish Museum, 1994.

1995   Cotter, Holland. "Feminist Art: 1962 until Tomorrow Morning and International." *New York Times*,
            17 March 1995, p. C25.
        Demos, T. J. "Elaine Reichek." *New Art Examiner*, September 1995, pp. 45–46.
        Feldman, Melissa E. "Painting Supports My Ceramics Habit." *Women's Art Magazine*,
            September/October 1995, p. 12.
        Ferris, Alison. *Conceptual Textiles: Material Meanings.* Exh. cat. Sheboygan, Wis.: John Michael Kohler
            Arts Center, 1995.
        Fleming, Jeff. *Thread Bare: Revealing Content in Contemporary Art.* Exh. cat. Winston-Salem, N.C.:
            Southeastern Center for Contemporary Art, 1995.
        Hagen, Charles. "Elaine Reichek." *New York Times*, 12 May 1995, p. C23.
        Isaak, Jo Anna, Jeanne Silverthorne, and Marcia Tucker. *Laughter Ten Years After.* Exh. cat. Geneva, N.Y.:
            Hobart and William Smith Colleges Press, 1995.
        Marincola, Paula. "Fabric as Fine Art: Thinking across the Great Divide." *Fiberarts*, September/October
            1995, pp. 34–39.
        Massie, Annetta. "Postcolonial Kinderhood." Exh. brochure. Columbus, Ohio: Wexner Center for the
            Arts, 1995.
        "People and Ideas: All the Nude That's Fit to Print: Elaine Reichek and the *New York Times.*" *Aperture*,
            Winter 1995, p. 68.
        Reichek, Elaine. "Artist's Page." *Art Journal*, Spring 1995, pp. 12–13.
        Rimanelli, David. "Elaine Reichek." *New Yorker*, 22 May 1995, p. 19.
        Schjeldahl, Peter. "Gallery Legs." *Village Voice*, 30 May 1995, p. 81.
        Von Uslar, Rafael, and Irmtrud Wojak. *Zimmerdenkmäler.* Exh. cat. Essen, Germany: Klartext, 1995.
        Yee, Lydia. *Division of Labor: Women's Work in Contemporary Art.* Exh. cat. Bronx, N.Y.: Bronx Museum of
            the Arts, 1995.

1996   Chin, Mel. *Scratch.* Exh. cat. New York: Thread Waxing Space, 1996.
        Felshin, Nina. *Embedded Metaphor.* Exh. cat. New York: Independent Curators, Inc., 1996.
        Harrison, Helena A. "Artists Who Make Work Out of Play." *New York Times*, 7 January 1996, p. 10.
        Isaak, Jo Anna. *Feminism and Contemporary Art.* London, New York: Routledge, 1996.
        Isaak, Jo Anna, and Dan O'Connell. "Guests of the Nation." Exh. brochure. Philadelphia: Rosenwald-
            Wolf Gallery, University of the Arts, 1996.
        Kimmelman, Michael. "Too Jewish? Jewish Artists Ponder." *New York Times*, 8 March 1996, p. C29.
        Kleeblatt, Norman, et al. *Too Jewish.* Exh. cat. New York: The Jewish Museum, 1996.
        Ockman, Carol. "Too Jewish? Jewish Museum." *Artforum*, September 1996.
        Rimanelli, David. "Jewish Museum." *The New Yorker*, 3 June 1996, p. 16.
        ———. "Model Home." *The New Yorker*, 19 February 1996, p. 22.
        Rolo, Jane, and Ian Hunt. *Bookworks: A Partial History and Sourcebook.* London: Bookworks, 1996.
        Schneider, Arnd. "Uneasy Relationships: Contemporary Artists and Anthropology." *Journal of Material
            Culture*, July 1996, p. 186.
        Smith, Roberta. "Fine Art and Outsiders: Attacking the Barriers." *New York Times*, 9 February 1996,
            p. C18.
        Tucker, Marcia. *Labor of Love.* Exh. cat. New York: New Museum of Contemporary Art, 1996.

1997   De Salvo, Donna, and Annetta Massie. *Apocalyptic Wallpaper.* Exh. cat. Columbus, Ohio: Wexner Center
            for the Arts, 1997.
        Keiter, Ellen J. *Hanging by a Thread.* Exh. cat. Yonkers, N.Y.: Hudson River Museum of Westchester, 1997.
        Lineberry, Heather. *Art on the Edge of Fashion.* Exh. cat. Tempe, Ariz.: Arizona State University Art
            Museum, 1997.

McKenna, Kristine. "'Too Jewish?' Hardly." *Los Angeles Times*, 2 February 1997, pp. 5, 83.

St. Sauveur, Michelle de. "Embedded Metaphor." *New Art Examiner*, March 1997, p. 43.

1998   Archer, Michael. "Loose Threads." *Art Monthly*, October 1998, pp. 27–29.

Batchelder, Anne. "Hanging by a Thread." *Fiber Arts*, Summer 1998, p. 36–42.

Cooke, Lynne. *Arkipelag: Ethno-Antics.* Exh. cat. Stockholm, Sweden: Nordiska Museet, 1998.

Cork, Richard. "Saying It with Thread." *The Times* (London), 1 September 1998, p. 14.

Corrin, Lisa. *Loose Threads.* Exh. cat. London: Serpentine Gallery, 1998.

Cotter, Holland. "Messages Woven, Sewn or Floating in the Air." *New York Times*, 9 January 1998.

Ghelerter, Donna, and Ingrid Schaffner. "Cross Sampling: Elaine Reichek's Needlework." *Pink* 2, no. 7 (Spring 1998).

McGonagle, Declan. *The Collection of the Irish Museum of Modern Art.* Dublin: Irish Museum of Modern Art, 1998.

Teilhet-Fisk, Jehanne, et al. *Dimensions of Native America: The Contact Zone.* Exh. cat. Tallahassee, Fla.: Museum of Fine Arts, Florida State University, 1998.

Zimmer, Bill. "Works That Are Made from Textiles." *New York Times*, 18 January 1998.

1999   Arning, Bill. "Elaine Reichek's Rewoven Histories." *Art in America*, March 1999, pp. 90–95.

Bourbon, Matthew. "Elaine Reichek: Nicole Klagsbrun Gallery." *New York Arts Magazine*, February 1999.

Camhi, Leslie. "Stitchcraft." *Village Voice*, 23 February 1999, p. 134.

Cotter, Holland. "New Samplers That Give Old Pieties the Needle." *New York Times*, 5 March 1999, p. E48.

Friis-Hansen, Dana. *Other Narratives.* Exh. cat. Houston, Tex.: Contemporary Arts Museum, 1999.

Handler, Beth. "New Exhibitions." *MoMA Magazine*, February 1999, p. 38.

———. "Projects 67: Elaine Reichek." Exh. brochure. New York: The Museum of Modern Art, 1999.

Kemmerer, Allison. *Referencing the Past: Six Contemporary Artists.* Exh. brochure. Andover, Mass.: Addison Gallery of American Art, Phillips Academy, 1999.

Newhall, Edith. "Talent: Stitch in Time." *New York Magazine*, 8 February 1999, p. 88.

Pollack, Barbara. "New York Reviews: Elaine Reichek." *Art News*, May 1999, p. 165.

Reichek, Elaine. "Endurance: A Project by Elaine Reichek." *New York Arts*, November 1999, pp. 48–51.

Rothbart, Daniel. "Reviews: Elaine Reichek." *New York Arts*, February 1999, p. 67.

Schwendener, Martha. "Projects 67: Elaine Reichek." *Time Out New York*, 18–25 March 1999, p. 63.

Sundell, Margaret. "Elaine Reichek: Museum of Modern Art/Nicole Klagsbrun Gallery." *Artforum*, Summer 1999, p. 155.